ADALENA KAVANAGH

ELISA GABBERT

The Unreality of Memory

Elisa Gabbert's previous collections of poetry, essays, and criticism include *The Word Pretty*, a *New York Times* Editors' Pick; *L'Heure Bleue, or The Judy Poems*; *The Self Unstable*, which was named one of the best books of 2013 in *The New Yorker*; and *The French Exit*. Her writing has appeared in *The New York Times Magazine*, *The New York Review of Books*, *The Guardian Long Read*, *London Review of Books*, *A Public Space*, *The Paris Review*, and many other publications. She lives in Denver.

ALSO BY ELISA GABBERT

ESSAYS

The Word Pretty

POETRY

L'Heure Bleue, or The Judy Poems

The Self Unstable

The French Exit

THE UNREALITY OF MEMORY

THE

UNREALITY

OF

MEMORY

And Other Essays

·

ELISA GABBERT

FSG ORIGINALS

Farrar, Straus and Giroux
New York

·

FSG Originals
Farrar, Straus and Giroux
120 Broadway, New York 10271

Owing to limitations of space, illustration credits can be found
on page 259.

Library of Congress Cataloging-in-Publication Data
Names: Gabbert, Elisa, author.
Title: The unreality of memory : and other essays / Elisa Gabbert.
Description: First edition. | New York : Farrar, Straus and Giroux, 2020. |
    Series: FSG originals | Includes bibliographical references.
Identifiers: LCCN 2020012311 | ISBN 9780374538347 (paperback)
Classification: LCC PS3607.A227 A6 2020 | DDC 814/.6—dc23
LC record available at https://lccn.loc.gov/2020012311

Designed by Abby Kagan

Our books may be purchased in bulk for promotional, educational, or
business use. Please contact your local bookseller or the Macmillan
Corporate and Premium Sales Department at 1-800-221-7945, extension
5442, or by e-mail at MacmillanSpecialMarkets@macmillan.com.

www.fsgoriginals.com • www.fsgbooks.com
Follow us on Twitter, Facebook, and Instagram at @fsgoriginals

1   3   5   7   9   10   8   6   4   2

For J

Let the disaster speak in you, even if it be by your forgetfulness or silence.
—MAURICE BLANCHOT, *The Writing of the Disaster*

With the inflation of apocalyptic rhetoric has come the increasing unreality of the apocalypse. A permanent modern scenario: apocalypse looms . . . and it doesn't occur. And it still looms.
—SUSAN SONTAG, *AIDS and Its Metaphors*

CONTENTS

PART THREE

PART

ONE

MAGNIFICENT DESOLATION

A couple of years ago, distracting myself at work, I saw a link on Twitter to a YouTube video that caught my attention. It was a computer-animated re-creation of the sinking of the *Titanic* in real time, all two hours and forty minutes of it. I did not watch the whole video, but I skipped around and watched parts, interested especially in the few interior views, where you can watch the water level slowly rising at an angle—since the ship pitched forward as it sank—in the white-painted hallways of the lower decks, and later, in the ballroom and grand staircase, as wicker chairs bob around.

The strangest thing about the video is that it includes no people—no cartoon passengers. There is no violin music, no voice-over. The ship is lit up, glowing yellow in the night, but the only sound, apart from a few emergency flares and engine explosions, is of water sloshing into and against the ship. The overall impression is of near silence. It's almost soothing.

This is true until the last few minutes of the video, when the half-submerged ship begins to groan and finally cracks in half. Only then, as the lights go out and the steam funnels collapse, do you hear the sound of people screaming, which continues for another thirty seconds after the ship has disappeared. A caption on the screen reads: "2:20—Titanic is gone. Rescue does not arrive for another hour and forty minutes." A few lifeboats (empty) are seen floating on the calm black ocean, under a starry sky. Then, another caption: "2:21—Titanic is heard beneath the surface breaking apart and imploding as it falls to the sea floor." The video ends on this disturbing note, with no framing narrative to lend a pseudo-happy ending.

At once, I was obsessed with the story of the *Titanic*. I rewatched the James Cameron movie (which I first saw in high school—still ridiculous, still gripping); I read a Beryl Bainbridge novel (*Every Man for Himself*) based on the night of the sinking, which felt like a novelization of the Cameron movie, though the book predates it, just; I read thousands of words on Wikipedia and what you might call fan sites, if you can be a fan of a disaster—lists of "facts" and conspiracy theories. I watched a documentary (*Titanic's Final Mystery*) about a weird new theory of the root cause of the disaster: One scientist thinks that a sudden and extreme drop in temperature caused a mirage on the horizon that obscured the iceberg from the men in the lookout until they were nearly upon it. The same illusion could explain why a nearby ship, the SS *Californian*, did not see that the *Titanic* was clearly in distress. It is, of course, just a theory.

The Hollywood version of the narrative, which puts the blame on hubris, has a lot of pull—the *Titanic* sank because they dared to call it unsinkable. It's the Icarus interpretation: Blinded by a foolhardy overconfidence, we flew too close to the sun, melting our wings, and so on. It's the easiest explanation, appealing in its simplicity, its mythic aura.

When I ran out of freely available *Titanic* material, I moved on to other disasters. I had an overwhelming desire for disaster stories, of a particular flavor: I wanted stories about great technological feats meeting their untimely doom. I felt addicted to disbelief—to the catharsis of reality denying my expectations, or verifying my worst fears, in spectacular fashion. The obvious next stop was 9/11.

So far, 9/11 is the singular disaster of my lifetime. People who were in New York City at the time always comment on how "beautiful" and "perfect" that September morning was, with "infinite visibility"—pilots call those conditions "severe clear." As I recall, it was a bright blue day in Houston too. I was driving from my apartment to the Rice University campus a couple of miles away when I heard radio reports of a plane hitting one of the Twin Towers. I continued driving to school, parked my car in the stadium lot, and went into the student center, where a few people were watching the news on TV with that air of disbelief that can appear almost casual.

The live footage of a massive steel skyscraper with smoke pluming from a hole in its side was shocking, but I felt it dully—shock in the form of incomprehension, maybe denial. I don't remember truly feeling horror—that is, understanding—until people began to jump from the buildings. They were specks against the scale of the towers, filmed from a distance, but you knew what they were. They became known as the "jumpers": people trapped in the upper floors of the buildings, above the planes' impact and unable to get out, who were driven to such desperation from the extreme heat and lack of oxygen that they broke the thick windows with office furniture and jumped to the pavement hundreds of stories below. Leslie E. Robertson, the lead structural engineer of the towers, later wrote that "the temperatures above the impact zones must have been unimaginable." The people nearby, and still in the buildings, could hear the bodies landing.

An Associated Press photo dubbed "The Falling Man" captures one of these jumpers: a man "falling," as if at ease, upside down and in parallel with the vertical grid of the tower. (It's a trick of photography; other photos in the series show him tumbling haphazardly, out of control.) The photo was widely publicized at first but then met with vehement critique. Some people found this particular image too much to take, an insult to their senses. And though the jumps were witnessed by many, the New York City medical examiner's office classifies all deaths from the 9/11 attacks as homicides. Of course, the deaths were forced, forced by suffering—but they were also voluntary. It seems akin to prisoners held in solitary confinement (or otherwise tortured) killing themselves—murder by suicide.

When I think of the jumpers, I think of two things. I think of images of women covering their mouths—a pure

expression of horror. They were caught on film, watching the towers from the streets of Manhattan. I do this sometimes—hand up, mouth open—when I see or read something horrible, even when alone. What is it for? I think, too, of the documentary about Philippe Petit, who tightrope-walked between the tops of the towers in 1974. At the time, they were the second-tallest buildings in the world, having just been surpassed by the Sears Tower in Chicago. It was an exceptionally windy day (it's always windy at 1,300 feet) and when a policeman threatened him from the roof of one building, Petit danced and pranced along the rope, to taunt him. This feels like one of the craziest things a man has ever done. For the jumpers, death was not a risk but a certainty; they jumped without thinking. It's more horrible to contemplate than many of the other deaths because we know the jumpers were tortured. Death is more fathomable than torture.

A Discovery Channel documentary that I found on YouTube called *Inside the Twin Towers* provides a minute-by-minute account of the events on September 11, a mix of reenactments and interviews with survivors. One man who managed to escape from the North Tower—he was four floors below the impact—recounts a moment when he opened a door and saw "the deepest, the richest black" he had ever seen. He called into it. Instead of continuing down the hall to see if anyone was there, he retreated back to his office in fear. He says in the film, "If I had gone down the hallway and died, it would have been better than living with this knowledge of 'Hey, you know what, when it came right down to it, I was a coward.' And it was actually our two coworkers down that hallway, on the other side, that ended up dying on that day. And I often think now, Perhaps I should have continued down that hallway."

This is a classic case of survivor's guilt, sometimes known as concentration-camp syndrome: the sense that your survival is a moral error. Theodor Adorno, in an amendment to his somewhat misunderstood line about poetry after Auschwitz, wrote:

> Perennial suffering has as much right to expression as a tortured man has to scream; hence it may have been wrong to say that after Auschwitz you could no longer write poems. But it is not wrong to raise the less cultural question whether after Auschwitz you can go on living—especially whether one who escaped by accident, one who by rights should have been killed, may go on living. His mere survival calls for the coldness, the basic principle of bourgeois subjectivity, without which there could have been no Auschwitz; this is the drastic guilt of him who was spared. By way of atonement he will be plagued by dreams such as that he is no longer living at all.

This syndrome, along with post-traumatic stress disorder, goes some way toward explaining why so many Holocaust survivors have committed suicide.

———

There is survivor's guilt, but there is also survivor's elation, survivor's thrill—a thrill felt only by those a little farther from disaster. The September 24, 2001, issue of *The New Yorker* included a symposium of responses to the attacks. A few were able to acknowledge the element of thrill in observation. Jonathan Franzen wrote:

> Unless you were a very good person indeed, you were probably, like me, experiencing the collision of several incompatible worlds inside your head. Besides the horror and sadness of what you were watching, you might also have felt a childish disappointment over the disruption of your day, or a selfish worry about the impact on your finances, or admiration for an attack so brilliantly conceived and so flawlessly executed, or, worst of all, an awed appreciation of the visual spectacle it produced.

I find Franzen's moral hierarchy here questionable, that "worst of all" most puzzling. Because to me, more than worry, or admiration (!), the most natural and undeniable of reactions would seem to be awe.

It's the spectacle, I think, that makes a disaster a disaster. A disaster is not defined simply by damage or death count; deaths by smoking or car wrecks are not a disaster because they are meted out, predictable. A disaster must not only blindside us, but be witnessed, and re-witnessed, in public. The *Challenger* explosion killed only seven people, but like the *Titanic*, which killed more than 1,500, and like 9/11, which killed almost 3,000, the deaths were both highly publicized and completely unexpected. Disasters are news because they are news.

All three of these incidents forced people to watch huge man-made objects, monuments of engineering, fail catastrophically, being torn apart or exploding in the sky. These are events we rarely see except in movies. The destruction of the *Challenger* and the World Trade Center are now movies themselves, clips we can watch again and again. The ubiquity of cameras, which we now carry all the time in our pockets, makes disaster easier to witness and to reproduce; it may even create a kind of cultural demand for disasters. We also get to watch the reaction shots—both the special effects and the human drama.

Roger Angell's version of survivor's thrill in the same *New Yorker* issue is less chastising:

> When the second tower came down, you cried out once again, seeing it on the tube at home, and hurried out onto the street to watch the writhing fresh cloud lift above the buildings to the south, down at the bottom of this amazing and untouchable city, but you were not surprised, even amid such shock, by what you found in yourself next and saw in the faces around you—a bump of excitement, a secret momentary glow. Something is happening and I'm still here.

Angell is saying this is not an aberration; it is the norm. It is one of the terrible parts of disaster, our complicity: the way we glamorize it and make it consumable; the way the news turns disasters into ready-made cinema; the way war movies, which mean to critique war, can really only glorify war.

We don't talk about it now, but I always found the Twin Towers hideously ugly, in a way not explainable by their shape alone—they were long rectangular prisms, nothing more. Their basic boxiness was somehow an affront. I find the Empire State Building and the Chrysler Building beautiful. I find the Eiffel Tower beautiful. It must be their tapering sweep, the way they diminish as they ascend, their detail suggesting fragility. How could anyone ever have found the Twin Towers beautiful? They seemed designed only to represent sturdiness, like campus buildings in the brutalist tradition that were said to be riot-proof.

A friend, a New Yorker, disagrees. She tells me the buildings "did amazing things with the light." Another, also from New York, says they were "sexy at night." But all skyscrapers are sexy at night, from below if not from afar, by virtue of their sheer dizzying size, their sheer *sheerness*. They stand like massive shears, stabbed into the sky.

Despite their imposing, even ominous height, the towers fell in less than two hours; the *Titanic* took only a little longer to sink. But that happened gradually. When you watch a building collapse, it seems like it suddenly *decides* to collapse. It's a building, and then it's not a building, just a crumbling mass of debris. There is no transition between cohesion and debris. It is terrifying how quickly an ordered structure dissolves. Where does it all go? Buildings, like anything, are mostly empty space.

In the vocabulary of disaster, the word "debris" is important—from the French *debriser*, to break down. A cherishable word, it sounds so light and delicate. But the World Trade Center produced hundreds of millions of tons of it. The bits of paper falling around the city led some people to mistake the attack for a parade. In space flight, or even on high-speed jets, tiny bits of foreign object debris (FOD) can cause catastrophe. Space food is coated in gel-atin to prevent crumbs, which in a weightless environment could work into vulnerable instruments or a pilot's eye. Debris on the runway could get sucked into a jet engine and cause it to fail.

The *Challenger* explosion, like the sinking of the *Titanic*, is usually chalked up to hubris. But if hubris is overconfidence—"presumption toward the gods"—the ex-planation is unsatisfying. Engineers at NASA's Marshall Space Flight Center knew that the O-ring seals, which helped contain hot gases in the rocket boosters, were poorly designed and could fail under certain conditions—conditions that were present on the morning of the launch, which was unusually cold. The O-rings were designated as "Criticality 1," meaning their failure would have cat-astrophic results. But the engineers did not take action to ground all shuttle flights until the problem could be fixed. As the very first sentence in the official *Report of the Presidential Commission on the Space Shuttle* Challenger *Accident* puts it: "The Space Shuttle's Solid Rocket Booster problem began with the faulty design of its joint and increased as both NASA and contractor management first failed to recognize it as a problem, then failed to fix it and finally treated it as an acceptable flight risk." What shocks me most when I read about the space program is the magnitude of the risks. The *Challenger* exploding on live TV in front of 17 percent of Americans was unthinkable to most of those viewers, but not unthinkable to workers at NASA.

From what I understand, NASA has always embraced risk. In his memoir *Spaceman*, the astronaut Mike Massimino, who flew on two missions to service and repair the Hubble telescope, recounts the atmosphere at NASA after the space shuttle *Columbia* broke up on reentry in 2003:

> When I walked in I saw Kevin Kregel in the hallway. He was standing there shaking his head. He looked up and saw me. "You know," he said, "we're all just playing Russian roulette, and you have to be grateful you weren't the one who got the bullet." I immediately thought about the two *Columbia* missions getting switched in the flight order, how it could have been us coming home that day. He was right. There was this tremendous grief and sadness, this devastated look on the faces of everyone who walked in. We'd lost seven members of our family. But underneath that sadness was a definite, and uncomfortable, sense of relief. That sounds perverse to say, but for some of us it's the way it was. Space travel is dangerous.

People die. It had been seventeen years since *Challenger*. We lost *Apollo 1* on the launch pad nineteen years before that. It was time for something to happen and, like Kevin said, you were grateful that your number hadn't come up.

The culture of risk at NASA is so great that in place of survivor's guilt there is only survivor's relief. But knowing the risks and doing it anyway must require some level of cognitive dissonance. This is apparent when Massimino writes that "like most accidents, *Columbia* was 100 percent preventable." This is hindsight bias; only past disasters look 100 percent preventable. The *Columbia* shuttle broke apart due to damage inflicted on the wing when a large chunk of foam insulation flew into it during launch. This was observed on film, and the ground crew questioned whether it might have caused any damage. However, insulation regularly broke apart during launches and had never caused significant damage before. Further, NASA determined that even if the spacecraft had been damaged, which it had no way of verifying, there was nothing that the flight crew could do about it, so NASA officials didn't even inform them of the possibility of the problem.

When *Columbia* came apart during reentry, disintegrating and raining down parts like a meteor shower over Texas and Louisiana, an investigation was launched. At first, no one believed that the foam could have done enough damage to cause the accident. It was "lighter than air." Massimino writes, "We looked at the shuttle

hitting these bits of foam like an eighteen-wheeler hitting
a Styrofoam cooler on the highway." Not until they actually reenacted the event by firing a chunk of foam at five
hundred miles per hour toward a salvaged wing and saw
the results did they accept it as the cause of the disaster.
Anything going that fast has tremendous force. This was
not like the failure of the O-ring; the risks of the insulation were not understood. Or, more properly, they were
simply not seen—it's basic, though unintuitive, physics.
The same type of accident is 100 percent preventable now
only because the disaster happened, triggering a shuttle re-
design. When redesigns cost billions of dollars, if it isn't
broke, they don't and probably can't fix it.

The concept of hubris lets us off too easy. It allows us to
blame past versions of ourselves, past paradigms, for faulty
thinking that we've since overcome. But these scientists we
might scoff at now were incredibly smart and incredibly
well prepared. The number of things that *didn't* go wrong
on all the space missions is astounding. It's easy to blame
people for not thinking of everything, but how could they
think of everything? How can we?

Not knowing the unknowable isn't hubris. There is
danger in thinking, "We were dumb then, but we're smart
now." We *were* smart then, and we *are* dumb now—both
are true. We do learn from the past, but we can't learn
from disasters we can't even conceive of. While disasters
widen our sense of the scope of the possible, there are limits. We can't imagine all possible futures. Yet we call this
hubris. Perhaps it's comforting to believe that disasters are

the result of some fixable "fatal flaw," and not an inevitable part of the unfolding of history.

To say there are limits to technological progress—we can't prepare ourselves completely for the unforeseen—is not to say that progress is impossible, but that progress is tightly coupled with disaster. As the French cultural theorist Paul Virilio famously said, "The invention of the ship was also the invention of the shipwreck." Not until we experience new forms of disaster can we understand what it is we need to prevent. Overreliance on the explanatory power of hubris is itself a form of hubris, a meta-hubris. And without hubris pushing us, however blinkered, forward, would there be any progress at all? Don't we need hubris to enable and justify advances in technology? NASA seems to take hubris in stride; they see occasional disaster as the fair cost of spaceflight.

In his "Letter from Birmingham Jail," Martin Luther King, Jr., warned of "the strangely irrational notion that there is something in the very flow of time that will inevitably cure all ills." You could say the same of technological progress; it is tempting to believe that progress occurs on a linear curve, that eventually all problems will be solved, and all accidents will be completely preventable. But there's no reason to assume that the curve of progress is linear, that the climb is ever increasing.

I want to come back to the *Titanic*, and some common misconceptions. One is that there were not enough lifeboats on board for frivolous reasons—because proprietors felt they would look unattractive on deck, or because they were regarded as mere symbols, serving only to comfort nervous passengers on a ship designers believed was literally unsinkable. This isn't the case. Rather, the thinking at the time was that the safest method of rescue, in the event of an emergency, was to ferry passengers back and forth between the sinking ship and a rescue ship. Because the *Titanic* would sink slowly, if at all, people would actually be safer on the ship, for some time, than in a lifeboat. Therefore, the lifeboats didn't need to accommodate the entire capacity of the ship in one go.

So why did the *Titanic* sink so fast? The surprising truth is that if the ship had hit the iceberg head-on, instead of narrowly missing it at the stern and then scraping along its side, it would not have sunk. The ship was capable of sustaining major damage from an impact like an iceberg— it could have stayed afloat if four of its sixteen watertight bulkheads were flooded. But the iceberg tore into the ship in such a way that five compartments were damaged. This event was not, realistically, foreseeable; no iceberg in history had done that kind of damage to a ship, and none has done that kind of damage since. It was, in essence, a freak accident.

There are echoes of this in the World Trade Center's collapse. It's well-known that the buildings were designed to survive the impact of an airplane. However, the engineers were envisioning emergencies like a small, slow-flying plane hitting one of the towers by accident—in fact, a bomber flying in near-zero visibility had hit the Empire State Building in 1945—not a modern jet being flown purposely into a tower at top speed. Still, there was a false sense of security. After the first impact, the PA system in the building told people to remain at their desks when of course they should have been evacuating. Some building staff also told workers it would be safer to stay where they were.

Is this hubris, or something else? Disasters always feel like a thing of the past. We want to believe that better technology, better engineering will save us. That the more information we have, the safer we can make our technology. But we can never have all the information. In creating new technology to address known problems, we unavoidably create new problems, new unknowns. Progress changes the parameters of possibility. This is something we *strive* for—to innovate past the event horizon of what we can imagine. And with so much that is inaccessible, opaque, and in flux, we can't even hold on to what we already know.

As they stepped out of the lunar module and began their moon walk, Neil Armstrong said to Buzz Aldrin, "Isn't that something! Magnificent sight out there." Aldrin's cryptic, poetic response was "Magnificent desolation." I think of this quote when I see footage of disasters. Especially after years of buffer, years of familiarity, have lessened the sting, it's easy to see these events as, in their way, magnificent.

Magnificent creations beget magnificent failures. It is awesome that we built them; it was awesome when they fell. Horror and awe are not incompatible; they are intertwined.

Is it perversity or courage that allows some people to admit to survivor's thrill? On the afternoon of September 11, I remember meeting my then boyfriend on campus for lunch. He was a contrarian type, but his reaction still disturbed me—he was visibly giddy, buzzed by the news. It's not that I don't believe other people were excited, but no one else had revealed it. In 2005, before the levees broke in New Orleans, a friend of mine asked if I wasn't just a little bit disappointed that Hurricane Katrina hadn't turned out as bad as predicted. Just hours later, she regretted saying it.

Often, when something bad happens, I have a strange instinctual desire for things to get even worse—I think of a terrible outcome and then wish for it. I recognize the pattern, but I don't understand it. It's as though my mind is running simulations and can't help but prefer the most dramatic option—as though, in that eventuality, I could enjoy it from the outside. Of course, my rational mind knows better; it knows I don't want what I want. Still, I fear this part of me, the small but undeniable pull of disaster. It's something we all must have inside us. Who can say it doesn't have influence? This secret wish for the blowout ending?

2016

DOOMSDAY PATTERN

On May 31, 1945, U.S. Secretary of War Henry Stimson called a meeting of experts to advise President Harry Truman on the atomic bomb: Should we use it or not? J. Robert Oppenheimer, the scientist heading the Manhattan Project, was asked to explain the difference between the new bombs and the firebombs already in use. That spring, General Curtis LeMay had been firebombing Japan with napalm, a highly flammable and "sticky" mixture of gasoline and gelling agents. Almost a million people in sixty cities were "scorched, boiled, and baked to death," in LeMay's own words, in these napalm raids. It must have been hard to believe that the A-bomb could be dramatically more deadly—so what would it accomplish?

Oppenheimer's response was that anything living within two-thirds of a mile of the atomic bomb's blast site would be irradiated, and further, the *appearance* of the explosion would have its own impact. The meeting notes read: "It was pointed out that one atomic bomb on an arsenal would not be much different from the effect caused by any Air Corps strike of present dimensions. However, Dr. Oppenheimer stated that the visual effect of an atomic bombing would be tremendous."

At the time, this was purely theoretical. But six weeks later, Oppenheimer was present for the Trinity test, the first detonation of a nuclear weapon, in the desert of New Mexico. On that early morning of July 16, 1945, after an incredibly bright explosion (witnesses without eye protection were temporarily blinded), the light turned white, then red, then purple. This "purple luminescence," the effect of ionized atmosphere, smelled like a waterfall. The physicist Robert Serber said that "the grandeur and magnitude of the phenomenon were completely breathtaking."

The people who worked on the bomb understood that some of its power was symbolic—that the difference between nuclear warfare and previous classes of weaponry was partly aesthetic. Stimson even worried that the power of the symbol might be lost if the bomb were dropped on an already devastated country. He wrote in his diary, "I was a little fearful that before we could get ready the Air Force might have Japan so thoroughly bombed out that the new weapon would not have a fair background to show its strength." But Oppenheimer was right about the tremendous effect. The bombs the United States dropped on Hiroshima and Nagasaki felt qualitatively different, even if, in the end, the death toll didn't match that of the firebombs. As Laurens van der Post, then a prisoner of war in Japan, said, there was "something supernatural" about the atomic blasts.

I've often heard that the residents of Hiroshima were warned about the bomb—that the military dropped leaflets on the city instructing them to evacuate. This is something of a myth. The warnings were vague and not specific to any particular city; LeMay had been dropping leaflets with lists of possible bomb targets for weeks. Although the people of Hiroshima were preparing for attack, they had expected more firebombing and were clearing out fire lanes. They heard air-raid sirens on the morning of August 6, but they heard those every morning. They were not prepared for an entirely new kind of weapon, and the new kind of terror it would bring. As M. Susan Lindee puts it in *Suffering Made Real: American Science and the Survivors at Hiroshima*, "They had been eating an orange, working in a garden, or reading a book. Minutes later they wandered, without feeling, past corpses, neighbors trapped in burning mounds of rubble, or children without skin."

The Japanese word for the survivors of the bombings at Hiroshima and Nagasaki is *hibakusha*. This is not the word for "survivor." It is usually translated as "bomb-affected people" or "explosion-affected persons"—a euphemism, almost politically correct. They avoid the more direct term *seizonsha* ("survivors") because, as John Hersey writes in *Hiroshima*, "in its focus on being alive it might suggest some slight to the sacred dead."

This sounds well intentioned, but for all its sensitivity

toward the departed, the term in practice placed a stigma on the living, who were feared and considered unclean. The Wikipedia page for *hibakusha* shows a woman with black cross-hatchings on her back and arms—the pattern of the kimono she was wearing burned into her skin. The *hibakusha* were not inclined to identify themselves as such

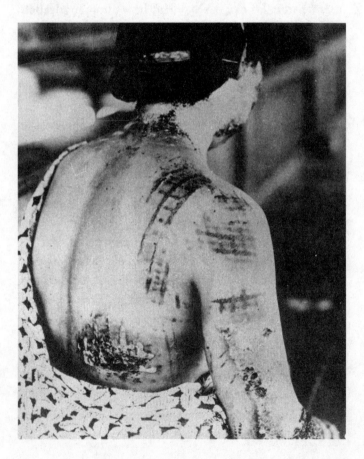

because it made them less employable and marriageable. There was little financial incentive either, since the Japanese government didn't offer the victims health care or other compensation until 1957.

I read *Hiroshima* in junior high, and the detail I always remembered most clearly from Hersey's account of the *hibakusha* was that their eyeballs melted. Those words, that image. I have remembered and re-remembered it so many times—*their eyeballs melted*—that I started to think it was a false memory, an invention of my imagination. It seems possible only as a metaphor, but it isn't. On page 51:

> On his way back with the water, he got lost on a detour around a fallen tree, and as he looked for his way through the woods, he heard a voice ask from the underbrush, "Have you anything to drink?" He saw a uniform. Thinking there was just one soldier, he approached with the water. When he had penetrated the bushes, he saw there were about twenty men, and they were all in exactly the same nightmarish state: their faces were wholly burned, their eyesockets were hollow, the fluid from their melted eyes had run down their cheeks. (They must have had their faces upturned when the bomb went off; perhaps they were anti-aircraft personnel.)

This passage informed my entire conception of war. For decades, I have found it difficult to accept that the bombs were necessary. The logical argument has trouble competing with the emotional impact of that etched-in detail.

Now, in its one-sidedness, the little yellow paperback
with a red sun on the cover has the whiff of propaganda—
but propaganda about what? Is it against nukes or war in
general? Was the *war* necessary? Chillingly, I've had the
same feeling, that I'm looking at propaganda, in Holocaust
museums. How are we to compare these two horrors, if it's
even possible? Am I supposed to choose sides?

Reading about the Hiroshima and Nagasaki attacks, I
see propaganda everywhere—Axis or Allies, pro- or anti-
war. The persistent belief that the cities were warned—isn't
that American propaganda? A kind of victim-blaming, as
in, they had their chance to escape? In the month before
the attacks, Truman wrote in his diary (I'm almost touched
that these men of war kept diaries):

> Even if the Japs are savages, ruthless, merciless and fa-
> natic, we as the leader of the world for the common wel-
> fare cannot drop this terrible bomb on the old Capitol
> or the new . . . The target will be a purely military one
> and we will issue a warning statement asking the Japs to
> surrender and save lives. I'm sure they will not do that,
> but we will have given them the chance.

This reads like rationalization, like self-propaganda: They
deserve it, even if they don't deserve it. We can't do it, but
we will. Later, after the bombing on August 6, Truman
would say over the radio, "It is an awful responsibility that
has come to us. Thank God it has come to us instead of
our enemies, and we pray that He may guide us to use it

in His ways and for His purposes." When the journalist Wilfred Burchett visited Hiroshima in September 1945, he described the symptoms of acute radiation sickness (severe nausea, vomiting, and diarrhea; swollen, bleeding tissue; hair loss) and called it "atomic plague." American scientists thought this was Japanese propaganda; they believed that if you were close enough to be irradiated, you'd be dead.

In 1980, *The New York Review of Books* published a letter to the editors and a response to that letter under the title "Was the Hiroshima Bomb Necessary?" In 1981, Paul Fussell wrote that it was "surely an unanswerable question." This was in an essay first published in *The New Republic* as "Hiroshima: A Soldier's View," which Fussell later retitled "Thank God for the Atom Bomb." It is written largely as a response to the "canting nonsense" of moralists "who dilate on the special wickedness of the A-bomb droppers." Fussell notes that most of the people who feel the use of the atomic bomb was wrong were not lined up for combat in Japan, as he was ("the farther from the scene of horror, the easier the talk"), and goes to some lengths to disabuse the reader of any idea that wartime in the pre-nuclear era was less horrific. He describes marines "sliding under fire down a shell-pocked ridge slimy with mud and liquid dysentery shit into the maggoty Japanese and USMC corpses at the bottom, vomiting as the maggots burrowed into their own foul clothing." He quotes Glenn Gray, a veteran and author, who wrote, "When the news of the atomic bombing of Hiroshima and Nagasaki came, many an American soldier felt shocked and ashamed." Fussell's response: "Shocked, OK, but why ashamed? Because we'd destroyed civilians? We'd been doing that for years." (In Errol Morris's film *The Fog of War*, Defense Secretary Robert McNamara, who helped plan the firebombing strategy, said LeMay once told him that if the United States had lost the war, he and the others involved would have been prosecuted as war criminals. McNamara wondered, "But what makes it immoral if you lose and not if you win?")

Fussell's aim in writing this provocative essay, he later explained, was "to complicate, even mess up, the moral picture," which he felt had been oversimplified by the "historian's tidy hindsight." He quotes various men of war: John Fisher, British admiral of the fleet: "Moderation in war is imbecility." Sir Arthur Harris, marshal of the Royal Air Force: "War is immoral." General William Tecumseh Sherman: "War is cruelty, and you cannot refine it." Louis Mountbatten, admiral of the fleet: "War is crazy." General George S. Patton: "War is not a contest with gloves. It is resorted to only when laws, which are rules, have failed." If we follow these arguments, there can be no war crimes— war is war, and the only objective is to kill more of them than they kill of us. War must be total.

However, Fussell's arguments seem to follow from a premise that he does not complicate or question: "The purpose of the bombs was not to 'punish' people but to stop the war." In this, he says, they were effective; they prevented further land invasions that might have killed him, an American. But it's far from an undisputed point.

Eisenhower thought nuclear weapons were "completely unnecessary," and a postwar analysis by the U.S. Strategic Bombing Command determined that Japan would have surrendered anyway, with or without the bombs and even without more invasions. Craig Nelson writes in *The Age of Radiance*, "They had lost sixty cities; Hiroshima and Nagasaki were just numbers sixty-one and sixty-two. If they hadn't given up after losing Tokyo, after all, they certainly wouldn't because of Nagasaki." There is evidence that the bombs were used in part to justify their enormous cost, as well as to send a signal to the USSR—quite the power move.

Nukes, like poison gas, can end up killing your own men and not just your enemies, depending on which way the wind blows, so they don't make very good weapons of war. But in their theoretical potency, their supernatural mystique—Russia's Tsar Bomba has the force of 3,333 Little Boys, and there are more than enough nukes in existence to destroy all life on this planet—they work very well as weapons of fear. They function as a threat: of punishment by annihilation. As such, Nelson claims, the atomic bombs "did not signal the end of World War II" but "the start of the Cold War."

The coldness of a cold war depends on reciprocal threat, the idea that mutually assured destruction will act as a deterrent against either side actually deploying the weapons. If the system works, the nuclear weapons stay symbols, and we all agree to live in constant low-level fear: the pre-apocalypse. But this system of shared risk, known as "brinkmanship" (as in a willingness to go to the brink of war), works only if both parties are rational—if the "adversary is not suicidal," as Evan Osnos wrote in a 2017 piece in *The New Yorker*, "The Risk of Nuclear War with North Korea." It's not clear, however, that either adversary in this case, Donald Trump or Kim Jong Un, is rational. North Korea has been unsure how to interpret Trump's aggression. Osnos's guide, Pak Song Il, said, "He might be irrational—or too smart. We don't know."

When Osnos asked Pak if his country was really prepared for the possibility of nuclear attack, Pak seemed unfazed:

> "A few thousand would survive," Pak said. "And the military would say, 'Who cares? As long as the United States is destroyed, then we are all starting from the same line again.'" He added, "A lot of people would die. But not everyone would die."

Can any game theory of war account for this level of befogged daredevilism? It throws a wrench in the works of brinkmanship if mutually assured destruction is seen as a point in nuclear warfare's favor.

I must have been profoundly uninterested in the news as a child, because I have no direct memory of two major events of 1986 that now obsess me: the *Challenger* explosion and Chernobyl. Chernobyl is by general consensus the "worst" nuclear disaster in history. But what does "worst" mean? One assumes this is measured by the number of casualties, or perhaps some combination of the number of casualties and the cost of the damage. But you learn very quickly when you're reading about nuclear disasters that it's difficult to fact-check anything; sources contradict each other and even self-contradict. This is understandable when you consider that the nuclear energy industry was born out of the nuclear weapons industry; the Cold War military complex was naturally prone to secrecy, and the energy industry inherited a serious PR problem.

I have read over and over that Chernobyl was the worst/biggest/deadliest nuclear accident ever (of course not counting the bombings in Japan, which were intentional), but according to *The Age of Radiance*, it was "merely the fourteenth most lethal nuclear accident in USSR history"—Nelson cites, for example, a 1957 accident at a plutonium plant in the Urals that irradiated 270,000 people and 14,000 square miles of land. The other thirteen were kept under wraps until glasnost. I had difficulty finding more information on these deadlier-than-Chernobyl accidents. Our cultural calculus on what constitutes the "worst" disasters must include how much publicity they get.

In any case, the people most affected by Chernobyl were not aware of those earlier incidents; they had been told, and believed, that nuclear power was safe. In fact, the Chernobyl accident resulted from a series of mistakes made during a safety test. The plant operators were trying to determine if the plant could function properly in a power loss due to a nuclear attack. Unfortunately, Soviet nuclear plants at the time were designed to double as production facilities for weapons-grade plutonium, so instead of the usual containment shell designed to protect the environs from radiation leaks in a worst-case scenario, they had a removable lid that facilitated fuel changes.

When Chernobyl exploded, workers at the plant and in the nearby town of Pripyat experienced something very like the Trinity test: a purple-and-pink glow in the sky; a fresh, clean scent like ozone. "It was pretty," one witness said. They went out and watched it from their balconies like an L.A. sunset. If they were quite close, they tasted something metallic. You see this in reports of radiation exposure—a taste of metal, like tinfoil, or in one case, "a combination of metal and chocolate." Cancer patients receiving radiotherapy describe the same sensation. It's not the flavor of waves or particles but a phantom taste—a sign of nerve damage.

Workers who realized what had happened called their wives and provided instructions: Swallow iodine, wash your hair, wipe down the counters, throw out the rag. If there's laundry drying, put it back in the wash. (I was surprised to learn that some radiation is superficial; you can wash it away.) But those workers themselves and, later, the many, many soldiers and volunteers who were called on to put out the fires and clean up the accident—known as the liquidators—absorbed obscene amounts of radiation. Some could work for only forty seconds at a time before reaching the lifetime limit of exposure. According to *The*

Chernobyl Nuclear Disaster, a textbook-like account by
W. Scott Ingram, Chernobyl's director, Viktor Brukhanov,

> realized then that his closest assistants were in a con-
> dition of shock. He became even more alarmed when
> he asked a health worker that he encountered to take a
> reading of the radioactivity in the atmosphere. The in-
> struments measured radioactivity in units called rems.
> A reading of 3.6 rems was considered high. The health
> worker told Brukhanov that the needle went off the dial
> at 250 rems. In other words, most of the people in the
> building and on the grounds had received deadly doses
> of radiation.

The cleanup workers faced a troublesome choice:
The protective clothing was so heavy that it made them
move slowly, and it was hard to get in and out of the site of
the accident quickly. Many simply didn't wear it.

The people in the zone of evacuation were incapable
of processing the disaster. Life had not given them the
training. In *Chernobyl Prayer,* Svetlana Alexievich collects
three hundred pages of testimony from survivors—the *hibakusha* of Chernobyl, the "Chernobyl people." ("You've got
a wife, children. A normal sort of guy. And then, just like
that, you've turned into a Chernobyl person.") In a chapter
titled "The author interviews herself on missing history and
why Chernobyl calls our view of the world into question,"
Alexievich writes:

The night of April 26, 1986. In the space of one night we shifted to another place in history. We took a leap into a new reality, and that reality proved beyond not only our knowledge but also our imagination. Time was out of joint. The past suddenly became impotent, it had nothing for us to draw on; in the all-encompassing—or so we'd believed—archive of humanity, we couldn't find a key to open this door. Over and over in those days, I would hear, "I can't find the words to express what I saw and lived through," "Nobody's ever described anything of the kind to me," "Never seen anything like it in any book or movie."

When a tsunami rises over a city, or a plane flies into a skyscraper, we say it's "just like a movie." This suggests that disaster movies help us process disaster—it's the only exposure most of us get, outside of news clips, to deadly spectacles. There's no script or template for a novel disaster.

In *Survivor Café*, Elizabeth Rosner notes, "When I ask Holocaust survivors to tell me their stories, I notice them flinch at the word. It's as though 'story' implies something invented, a fairy tale." *Chernobyl Prayer* does not feel like a collection of stories, with structures imposed retroactively. It is simply people talking, relating their experience. Many speak of their fondness for jokes: "I don't like crying. I like hearing new jokes." Here's a good one:

There's a Ukrainian woman sells big red apples at the market. She was touting her wares: "Come and get them!

Apples from Chernobyl!" Someone told her, "Don't advertise the fact they're from Chernobyl, love. No one will buy them." "Don't you believe it! They're selling well! People buy them for their mother-in-law or their boss!"

The Chernobyl people don't like to dwell:

I was struck by the indifference with which people talked about the disaster. In one dead village, we met an old man. He was living all alone. We asked him, "Aren't you afraid?" And he answered, "Of what?" You can't be afraid the whole time, a person can't do that; some time goes by, and ordinary life starts up again.

There are dozens of comparisons to war—it was the closest available analogue. (Nuclear accidents are usually spoken of in terms of "Hiroshimas." It's become a unit of measurement.) "We'd grown used to the idea that danger could only come from war." "It was a real war, an atomic war." "Just like in 1937." "Instead of assault rifles they gave us spades." "Is this what nuclear war smells like? I thought war should smell of smoke." "They call it 'an accident,' 'a disaster,' but it was a war. Our Chernobyl monuments resemble war memorials."

If it was a war, it was a war with no clear enemy: "To answer the question of how we should live here, we need to know who was to blame. Who was it? The scientists, the staff at the power plant? Or was it us, our whole way of seeing the world?" Another:

At first, it was baffling. It all felt like an exercise, a game.

But it was genuine war. Nuclear war. A war that was a mystery to us, where there was no telling what was dangerous and what wasn't, what to fear and what not to fear. No one knew.

When Wilhelm Röntgen discovered X-rays in 1895, he named them X because they represented the unknown. This gets at what was, and is, so uncanny about radiation: You can't see it; you can only see its effects. One cameraman sent to film the scene at Chernobyl after the fact said, "It wasn't obvious what to film. Nothing was blowing up anywhere." But some people, it seems, are immune to this fear of the unseeable; they refused to evacuate or later returned to the contaminated land, the zone of exclusion, because, one said, "I don't find it as scary here as it was back there." They chose contamination over exile, the invisible over the visible threat. "This threat here, I don't feel it. I don't see it. It's nowhere in my memory. It's men I'm afraid of. Men with guns."

As a whole, Alexievich's book is stunning, but difficult to take. It is bookended with two long monologues from women who lost the loves of their lives in the accident. They watched their husbands become unrecognizable: "His nose got somehow out of place and three times bigger, and his eyes weren't the same anymore. They moved in opposite directions." He begs for a mirror and she refuses. "I just didn't want him to see himself, to have to remember what he looked like." The other woman was pregnant, and while she sat at her husband's bed in the hospital, the baby inside her absorbed radiation "like a buffer." It was born two weeks early and died within four hours.

In their gut-wrenching grief, these monologues remind me of Marie Curie's mourning journal:

> They brought you in and placed you on the bed . . . I kissed you and you were still supple and almost warm . . . Oh! How you were hurt, how you bled, your clothes were inundated with blood. What a terrible shock your poor head, that I had caressed so often, taking it in my hands, endured. And I still kiss your eyelids which you close so often that I could kiss them, offering me your head with the familiar movement which I remember today, which I will see fade more and more in my memory.

Pierre Curie, severely weakened from radiation exposure, had fallen in the street and had his head run over by a horse and carriage.

In 1989, a group of journalists from the *Chugoku Shimbun*, a newspaper based in Hiroshima, began writing a series of global investigative reports, now collected in a book called *Exposure: Victims of Radiation Speak Out*. One of these reports quotes an antinuclear activist in the Soviet Union: "All the radiation sufferers of the world have to unite!" Another details the phenomenon of "radiophobia": "To describe the state of mind whereby a person becomes paranoid about radiation and its effects, the Soviet media often uses the word *radiophobia*. It expresses the feelings of the Soviet people, who are torn between the truth as told to them by the government, and the rumors they hear through unofficial channels."

In the same way that the Japanese concept of *hibakusha* can be extended to survivors of any nuclear accident or attack, Soviet-style radiophobia can be found anywhere with nuclear power. Conspiracy theories bloom around nuclear technologies because there is so much misinformation and conflicting information. Paul Fussell supported the use of the atomic bomb—and he repeats the received notion that Hiroshima was properly warned before the attack—but *not* nuclear energy, or "the capture of the nuclear-power trade by the inept and the mendacious (who have fucked up the works at Three Mile Island, Chernobyl, etc.)." Is this radiophobia? Long-term studies of survivors in Japan, Ukraine, and Belarus have shown that ranges of exposure previously thought to be highly dangerous are only slightly dangerous—with incidences of cancer perhaps 5 percent higher than the normal population. (We all have some exposure to radiation through daily living, not just from X-rays but from ordinary activities like eating bananas or taking a walk.) The people most at risk in a nuclear disaster, it turns out, are emergency workers and children, who are especially prone to thyroid cancers.

But this doesn't tell us much about the psychological effects of exposure. After Chernobyl, many were diagnosed with "panic disorder" or something called "vegeto-vascular dystonia," terms that, like "hysterical," seem like

little more than dismissals, euphemisms for "crazy." A report of the International Atomic Energy Agency supposed
that "the designation of the affected population as 'victims' rather than 'survivors' has led them to perceive themselves as helpless, weak and lacking control over their
future." The nuances of the terminology reflect degrees
of stigma, but they influence stigma too—the names we
give to people's discomfort affect how uncomfortable those
people make us.

Other studies have shown elevated stress levels in populations exposed to nuclear accidents even years later (for example, those living near Three Mile Island). Hersey, when
he visited Hiroshima again forty years after the bombing,
described a "lasting A-bomb sickness" marked by weakness, fatigue, dizziness, digestive problems, and "a sense of
doom." We know that chronic stress is bad for the body; it
can lead to heart disease, diabetes, immune disorders, any
number of conditions that might kill you. Is that not real?
Is fear not real? There's a tension in the literature around
nuclear disasters, between the need to accurately describe
them as they are—a kind of nightmare sublime—and to balance out "hysteria" by presenting cold "facts." It's difficult
to reconcile the horror of nuclear disasters with our ability to
move on. Where "Chernobyl people" tell jokes, the Japanese say "Shikata ga-nai"—roughly, "It can't be helped."

I want to talk about the hibakusha without succumbing to fearmongering and nuclear phobia. So here's a fact:
There have been many more deaths, orders of magnitude

more, from accidents in the fossil-fuel industries than in nuclear energy. But I can't think of a particular accident with as much disaster capital as Chernobyl. In 2010, there were "the 33," the trapped coal miners in Chile, but they all survived and became heroes.

Why are some deaths more horrifying than others?

In the spring of 2013, I often drove north on Route 93 in Colorado from Golden to Boulder. It's a gorgeous, hilly route, through yellow-green grassy fields, with misty blue mountains on your left, but dangerous in the snow; I know someone who totaled their car on that road. It snowed a lot that spring, to a maddening degree, once or twice a week right up through the end of May, but the snow made it even more gorgeous and misty, and sometimes I saw herds of antelopes.

About midway between Golden and Boulder, you pass Rocky Flats on your right. This area housed a plant that made plutonium triggers for nuclear bombs; it closed in 1992. What was the plant is now a Superfund site. The plant's first accident occurred on September 11, 1957 (the same year as that mysterious accident in the Urals), with another major and nearly catastrophic fire on Mother's Day in 1969. Waste was found to be seeping into open fields. In 1970, airborne radiation was detected in Denver. But the unsafe conditions continued for years, until informants tipped off the EPA and FBI, triggering a raid in

1989. Where was our glasnost? The *hibakusha* of Colorado filed a lawsuit, but after twenty years it was denied.

Until recently, there was a bar across the street from the site called the Rocky Flats Lounge—a truly great bar, kind of a cowboy bar, with an open back so you could watch the sun set over the mountains to the west. There were horses in view. They had karaoke on the weekends, and I once heard the bartender, a woman, sing a devastating version of "Fake Plastic Trees." They sold T-shirts and tank tops bearing mushroom clouds and the words I GOT NUCLEAR WASTED AT ROCKY FLATS. The bar is now permanently closed; it kept catching on fire.

I'm telling you this because I keep thinking about it. I keep thinking about Hurricane Irma; there were upward of eighty Superfund sites in its path. What will become of them? The EPA is being dismantled. I keep thinking about Fukushima, the new *hibakusha* it created. Japan sees earthquakes and tsunamis all the time; they have a culture of disaster preparedness. But preparation takes time. Before 2011, most seismologists believed that earthquakes with magnitudes of higher than 8.4 weren't possible in Japan. Climate change accelerates natural disasters. Earthquakes can trigger tsunamis and volcanic eruptions, and volcanic eruptions and earthquakes can trigger tsunamis; global warming leads to increases in all three. You can't prepare for the worst-case scenario when the scenario keeps getting rapidly worse.

After we talked on Twitter about the Cold War, a writer

I know named Michael Farrell Smith sent me a link to a lyric essay he wrote that includes this snippet of faux dialogue, an apt depiction of life in the pre-apocalypse:

Q. Could you talk about the *Challenger* explosion in the context of the Cold War?

A. I . . . guess so. Well, all those shuttles were a product of the U.S./U.S.S.R. space race, for one thing. And after the *Challenger*, when Chernobyl exploded and burned three months later, it felt as if some doomsday pattern was beginning. *Everything was going to explode. Nothing was safe.* Of course, I was just a kid, and what did I know, the world's more-or-less fine.

I feel this way all the time now. Nothing is safe. Everything's fine.

2017

THREATS

I happened to be in Seattle when I read "The Really Big One," Kathryn Schulz's 2015 *New Yorker* feature about the devastating Pacific Northwest earthquake experts think could hit any day. I was traveling for work—a three-day trip—and eating dinner alone in a sushi bar two blocks from the waterfront, scrolling on my phone with my left hand, chopsticks in my right. (Seattle's weather in July is uncharacteristically perfect: The sun was streaming through the tall windows; it wouldn't set, and then gorgeously, until after 9:00 p.m.) When I got to the part where a FEMA worker says, "Our operating assumption is that everything west of Interstate 5 will be toast," I looked up and wondered if I could move up my flight.

"The Seattle earthquake," as I've come to think of this looming event, is particularly threatening because the associated fault line is a subduction zone—a place where two tectonic plates push against, and over, each other. Subduction zones (sometimes called "megathrusts") are capable of producing earthquakes with magnitudes of 9.0 or higher. They were responsible for the earthquakes that caused the 2011 tsunami in Japan, leading to the Fukushima nuclear meltdown, and the 2004 tsunami in Indonesia, which killed nearly a quarter of a million people—the deadliest tsunami in recorded history.

The geologist Charles Rubin, by studying caves near the coast of Indonesia, has discovered that Indian Ocean tsunamis don't strike on a schedule. His team dug into the cave floor and found that they could date past tsunamis by the layers of guano interspersed with sea sand. The pattern is irregular—sometimes there are long gaps of hundreds of years; at other times the tsunamis strike in clusters. There is no necessary reprieve before another tsunami hits. The Cascadia subduction zone in the Pacific Northwest, in contrast, is more periodic: There have been forty-one Cascadia earthquakes in the past 10,000 years, occurring roughly every 240 years. The last one, however, was in 1700—317 years ago.

Both will come again, in time—one is unpredictable, the other predictable but well overdue. Which is more frightening?

Cumbre Vieja, Spanish for "Old Summit," is a volcanic ridge in the Canary Islands that some people think could collapse into the ocean, generating a tsunami or, as the BBC once termed it, a "mega-tsunami." (Tsunamis can arise from impact events, like a landslide or an asteroid, or from earthquakes on the ocean floor.) I first heard about Cumbre Vieja when I moved to Boston in 2002 for graduate school. My boyfriend at the time informed me that if this island collapsed, we would have five or six hours' notice before the tsunami arrived in Boston. He formulated a plan: As soon as we heard the news, we should start walking west, wherever we were. We toyed with establishing a meeting place, but the most important thing was to move. Some models predicted that a Cumbre Vieja collapse could flood the East Coast up to sixteen miles inland.

I lived in Boston for ten years, and Cumbre Vieja did not collapse. I thought of it rarely during that decade. Recently, I learned that the research, originally published in 1999, is controversial; an article in *Science of Tsunami Hazards* indicated that landslides may occur more gradually. I now live in Denver, far from any coasts. I sometimes remark to my husband, John, who misses his native New England, that I feel relatively safe here—safe from coastal flooding and violent storms related to climate change, safe from California's earthquakes. "What about drought?" he says. "And the caldera?"

A caldera is a giant, crater-like depression where the earth has sunk in after an enormous underground pocket of magma releases pressure. There's one at Yellowstone— it's so large nobody saw it at first; it's almost as large as the park. And it's active. A geologist named Robert Smith has been working in Yellowstone for decades. In the 1970s, he noticed that the trees on the south side of Yellowstone Lake had become waterlogged. He resurveyed the area and found that the whole lake had been displaced. Between 1923 and 1977, the center of the caldera had risen two feet, relocating the lake. More recently, the center has fallen again. Based on the placement of excavated arrowheads, which would have been left along the coast of the lake, archaeologists have determined that the lake has been rising and falling for fifteen thousand years. It's as though the whole caldera is inhaling and exhaling.

The Yellowstone caldera is a supervolcano—the "really big one" of volcanoes. A single supervolcano eruption is a million times more powerful than Little Boy, the atomic bomb dropped on Hiroshima. The last time the Yellowstone supervolcano erupted, it was a thousand times bigger than Mount St. Helens, which blasted seven billion tons of rock from the side of the mountain, enough to bury Manhattan in fifty-five feet of debris. Supervolcanoes eject billions of cubic feet of ash, compared to millions ejected by a standard volcano. (It's worth remembering how much more than a million a billion is. If you made $1 billion last year, and paid a tax rate of 99 percent, you'd still have $10 million.)

We would have some warning if the Yellowstone caldera were about to blow. Volcanic eruptions begin with earthquakes, and a series of earthquakes over weeks or months would presage an eruption. However, even given a lead time of years, it would still be unlikely that we could adequately prepare for such an event. We would be able to evacuate the immediate area, of course, where pyroclastic flows of fast-moving rock, gas, and ash—what the volcanologist Bill McGuire describes as "an avalanche on steroids"—would essentially boil bystanders alive. (There's a map online where a big red circle blots out most of Wyoming and Montana; it's labeled KILL ZONE.)

But the effects would be far-reaching, in both time and space. Denver is in the "downwind" area, and within a day the ashfall could be deeper than three feet: a blizzard of ash. But wet ash is much heavier than wet snow. If stranded in the open, you could suffocate. People would lose power and water. Planes in flight might crash, and aircraft would be grounded, as in the aftermath of the 2010 eruption of Iceland's Eyjafjallajökull volcano. Disturbingly, volcanic ash isn't really ash; it's more like finely ground rock, but jagged, like tiny shards of glass. Even hundreds of miles from the volcano, it can cause an unsettling condition known as hypertrophic pulmonary osteoarthropathy. In 1971, the paleontologist Michael Voorhies chanced upon a site now known as the Ashfall Fossil Beds, in northeastern Nebraska. A rare lagerstätte, or exceptionally well preserved sedimentary deposit, the fossil beds revealed a mass grave of animals who died near a watering hole twelve million years ago. In the book *Supervolcano: The Catastrophic Event That Changed the Course of Human History*, the authors John M. Savino and Marie D. Jones describe the cause of this slow, painful death, a supervolcano nearly a thousand miles from the watering hole:

Once the ash got into their lungs, it combined with naturally occurring moisture in the lungs to form a kind of cement. Birds and turtles were the first species to die as their lungs filled up with sediment; musk deer and small carnivores were next. The larger animals were also having trouble breathing. Inside their bodies, their bones were growing abnormal patches of highly porous new bone matter, especially around the lower jaw and on the shafts of major limbs, as well as their ribs. This is evidence that they were not getting enough oxygen.

According to a *Naked Science* documentary I found on YouTube (clearly cut for TV—the video keeps showing the same simulation of a future Yellowstone blast over and over again, for viewers just joining us), "normal life within five hundred miles of the volcano would be impossible." And the worst impact would be months or years later, after crops have failed and livestock have perished.

Like an asteroid impact, a supervolcano can cause global cooling, forming an ash cloud that blocks the sun and leads to widespread famine. At this moment in history, when we're breaking new heat records every month and the permafrost is melting, global cooling doesn't sound so bad. But there's no way to know what the new base-line temperature would be, when and if that happened. A "mini ice age" in the 1300s has been tied to both volcanic and earthquake activity in Europe, as well as the bubonic plague—though there is debate over which caused which. Natural disasters might have led to famine, which in turn could have led to weakened immune systems, making pop-ulations more vulnerable to the plague; but, then again,

perhaps mass deaths from the plague in fact led to reforestation, which then led to subsequent global cooling.

While searching for information about volcanoes
and tsunamis from my local library, I discovered a series
of Choose Your Own Adventure–style books titled, for
example, *Can You Survive an Asteroid Strike?* The sub-
title on each book is *An Interactive Doomsday Adventure.*
I checked two of them out. In the preamble to *Asteroid
Strike*, the reader finds herself watching an alarming news
announcement on TV. A "Dr. Grady," Stanford astrophys-
icist, is being interviewed. The news anchor asks, "Aren't
we lucky that it's hitting water instead of land?" "No, no,
no," he answers. "If anything, that's worse." He continues:
"This impact will affect everyone on Earth. It will create a
tsunami 1 to 2 kilometers high. It will set off massive earthquakes worldwide, which will cause even more tsunamis."
The news anchor "goes white" and asks, "So people need to
get to high ground to be safe?"

> Grady sighs. "In the short term, I suppose so. But un-
> derstand, this changes everything. Flaming debris rain-
> ing down everywhere. Massive earthquakes rocking the
> entire planet. Rock, dust, and steam blanketing Earth.
> We're talking about nuclear winter."

I never read this kind of book as a kid, and my interactive doomsday adventure ended rather quickly. (Ad-
mittedly, asteroids are my fantasy death, but I'd prefer

to die at ground zero, on impact, not later, in failed survivor mode.) I make the "mistake" of stopping to help an injured man in a suit. He turns out to be the Speaker of the House. "You're one of the most powerful people in the country," I say. "How come you don't have your own car? Or helicopter?" The man waves his cell phone. "Lines are jammed." A reminder that sufficiently catastrophic conditions might equalize power.

I think back to the Boston Marathon bombing in 2013. I was already living in Denver, but John and I both had Boston area codes, and no landline. We couldn't place calls that afternoon. Recently, I tried to meet up with friends at the Albuquerque Balloon Fiesta, but in the enormous crowds none of our phones were working—calls would drop, texts wouldn't go through—and we couldn't find each other. This alone makes the prospect of a catastrophe more terrifying: How on earth would we find anyone?

How are we supposed to feel about these natural threats, both certain and vague? Does their inevitability even help us prepare for them? In *Waking the Giant*, a book about the ways climate change accelerates natural disasters, Bill McGuire writes:

Having seen the global warming problem coming for more than 100 years, then, it seems quite incredible that we have yet to act decisively in order to do something about it. Or maybe not so extraordinary. Humans, as individuals, as groups, and together as a society, seem to be hard-wired to respond quickly and effectively to a sudden threat, but not to a menace that makes itself known stealthily and over an extended period of time.

If this is true, we're like the proverbial frog in a pot of boiling water, lulled into inaction by the slowly rising temperature. We're poorly equipped to deal with so-called long emergencies. And how can we prepare for a threat so big we can't even imagine it? As the narrator of a Discovery Channel segment on Cumbre Vieja puts it, "There is a problem with all major natural catastrophes: Because we've never experienced these things, we don't think they're going to happen to us, so we ignore them."

Not long after I learned about the Seattle earthquake, I read another long *New Yorker* piece, about "the most dangerous dam in the world." Mosul Dam in Iraq was built on an unstable foundation and could kill up to a million and a half people if or, more likely, when it fails. "If there is a breach in the dam, there will be no warning," says Azzam Alwash, an Iraqi American civil engineer and adviser on the dam. "It's a nuclear bomb with an unpredictable fuse." And yet people in the nearby farming village of Wanke, which would end up under sixty feet of water, just don't think much about it.

This reminds me, too, of Chernobyl survivors, of the cleanup worker who said, "You can't be frightened the whole time, a person can't do that; some time goes by, and ordinary life starts up again." "Normalization" is incredibly normal, a way of coping with terror by resetting our default values. Life before impending disaster and life after unexpected disaster may both require a *la-la-la* mentality. Perhaps the villagers, in both Iraq and Belarus, are more rational not to worry: Why bother, when there's nothing you can do? Ignoring the threat may be your best strategy, if thinking about it is too much to bear.

Part of the reason Chernobyl people had difficulty processing what happened to them was because nothing had prepared them for it. Astronauts go through so many simulations—often in hyperconvincing virtual reality environments, before they actually get to space—that their responses become internalized; in a real emergency, they carry out procedures almost automatically. The astronaut David Wolf once told me that the training environments are so realistic now that "you feel like you're up in space again." Wolf nearly died in space in 1997, when an airlock failed while he was out on a spacewalk. After years of training, when it comes to the actual disaster, he said, "You know this is real—but you think it through as if you were in a simulation."

The residents near Chernobyl were baffled when cleanup workers dug up and destroyed their crops, even shot their pets. Many were more afraid of the crews than what the crews warned them about—the visible versus the invisible threat. ("There was no telling what was dangerous and what wasn't, what to fear and what not to fear. No one knew.") They also didn't know whom to blame—the staff at the plant? Science itself? Themselves, for trusting the scientists? It was a war with no enemy.

Ecological disasters create the conditions of war, while giving us no one to bargain with—no one to fight or beg mercy from. Science improves our predictive power, but those predictions are often just a preview of the coming brute reality. While they may go some way toward preparing us psychologically, they can't in themselves protect us.

Once on Twitter I saw a link to an article titled "Should We Feel Guilty About Gentrification? This Podcast Will Help You Decide." I laughed at the absurdity of listening to a podcast just to get help deciding whether or not to feel guilty. A few months later, I spotted a book at the library, on a rack of recently returned books, called *What Should We Be Worried About?* These seem to be real questions we're wrestling with—where do I focus my anxiety so that I can feel like a good citizen in an anxious society? We believe we need to worry about the right problems, even if we can't solve them.

Worry, like attention, is a limited resource; we can't worry about everything at once. That means most of us are worrying about immediate threats—like losing our jobs or our health care—rather than nebulous threats that may or may not manifest over thousands of years, even if those latter threats are ultimately the greater concerns. One way to conserve our worry, as it were, is to offload it onto others—experts who presumably know better than we do the appropriate level of fear, and when to apply it. This may be an effective means of reducing personal anxiety, but it doesn't necessarily make us safer. Before 2011, the year of the magnitude-9.0 Great East Japan Earthquake, most seismologists believed that earthquakes with magnitudes higher than 8.4 were not possible in Japan. This is why Japan, where earthquakes and tsunamis are common, was unprepared for the consequences.

With diseases, prevention is better than cure—there's no cure for polio, so we need the vaccine. But we can't prevent these kinds of disasters. Take the Yellowstone caldera—can we lessen the force of an eruption by drilling down into the magma chamber to release some of the pressure? Not at all. Even if you were able to overcome the technological challenge of drilling that far down, says Daniel Dzurisin, a geologist with the U.S. Geological Survey's Volcano Hazards Program, "all you would be doing is a pinprick, in a very large, very complicated system—it's not just a big balloon full of magma, and it wouldn't notice."

I love that formulation: *It wouldn't notice.* We can study a subduction zone obsessively, or we can pretend it doesn't exist. Millions of people who live in areas vulnerable to megathrust tsunamis don't even have the choice to worry or not; they don't know the threat exists to begin with. Especially now, when we're likely past the point of avoiding a climate calamity of our own creation, disasters can feel like karmic punishment. But the earth is not a vengeful god—just an indifferent one.

2017

BIG AND SLOW

The *Kelpies* are two enormous steel horse-head sculptures—they're a hundred feet high and weigh over three hundred tons—that were completed in 2013 and now live in a park in Scotland. The one on the left, when you're facing the sculptures, seems calm, or at least quiet; there's a hint of judgment, perhaps, in the set of the head, the squint of its eyes. The one on the right is throwing its head back, mouth parted, as though bucking and neighing, rearing up on its hind legs. The horses have no legs, but seen at a distance, from the right angle, it looks as if they're cresting the horizon, like they're running up over a hill—to kill you, probably, like the giant rabbits in *Night of the Lepus*. They call to mind the statues on Easter Island, which are not, it turns out, just heads; their bodies are buried, most of their mass below the surface.

The Kelpies, of course, are perfectly stationary, but they capture the essence of horses in movement. It's a little frightening, even in a photograph. When you do an image search on Google for "megalophobia"—the fear of large objects—one of the first results is a picture of *The Kelpies*. The sculptures and the phobia are tightly coupled in my mind: I learned of them at the same time. Under a tweet with a picture of the horses, shrouded in fog, looking terrifyingly real, a woman had replied that they "really triggered" her megalophobia. I felt an instant kind of antirecognition. I have a primal reaction to massive objects, but it's not a panicky fear, like my fear of heights. (I get heart palpitations walking over metal grates and high bridges.) And it's not a gross-out fear, as in trypophobia, the fear of irregular holes—a disgust reaction to images of coral and dried lotus pods. Instead, it's a tingly fear, a fetishistic pleasure, an attractive force.

I have scrolled through the megalophobia image results more than once, losing track of time. Many are from the megalophobia subreddit, where people post images of the enormous things that horrify them: scuba divers floating like hummingbirds next to giant jellyfish; wind turbines; the prows of massive ships, especially seen from below, to accentuate their looming; the space shuttle transporter; Hoover Dam. Some are illustrations, and some are fakes—maybe the jellyfish, certainly the dragons and spaceships. But most are real objects that dwarf the human scale, such as offshore drilling platforms, which look like inside-out factories mounted on aircraft carriers mounted on legs, legs that can extend eight or nine thousand feet underwater, a baffling depth. The megalophobia effect is best, perhaps, when there's a combination of manufactured and natural elements, which explains why many of the images are cross-posted to r/submechanophobia (the fear of submerged man-made objects). The ocean is the ultimate earthly object of unfathomable size, extending seemingly without limit in two directions at once, out to the horizon and down. We can't grasp the depth of the ocean until we throw a skyscraper down there.

After finding *The Kelpies*, I started my own minor collection of megalophobia images. I saw and saved a black-and-white photo of a towering rock formation on a beach (captioned on Twitter with "Possible novel structure"), a few tiny people on a sandbar below. The water caught all the light, while the rock face was almost featurelessly black, a silhouette in the shape of the *Titanic*. It must be natural, but it seemed dropped there, a monolith as in *2001*, uninterpretable. Looking at it feels like hearing a loud bass note on a piano, a singular note of doom.

In another from my collection, a photograph by Nadav Kander, a partially built bridge hangs in yellow mist; the ends of the bridge arc up from the shores of the wide Yangtze River, but the middle is missing. (It looks like a still from a recurring anxiety nightmare: I'm driving on an overpass and suddenly realize it ends in mid-air like a cliff.) There are cranes perched up there—construction cranes, not birds—on the unfinished edges.

Frozen like that, the bridge looks as if it will never be finished, like the Crazy Horse Memorial in South Dakota. It's intended to dwarf nearby Mount Rushmore when complete—according to the memorial's website, "The 563-foot-high Mountain Carving will dominate the horizon." If it ever is completed, it may be the world's largest sculpture. But for now it's a sad construction zone with little funding, and with far fewer visitors than Mount Rushmore. (When I pulled around a curve on the road and saw those four gigantic presidents' heads from a distance, I started laughing uncontrollably; they're so essentially stupid.)

I kept that broken-bridge photo open in a tab for several months. What is the fascination? Unlike photos of *The Kelpies*, what it and the rest of the artist's Yangtze River series depicts is frankly kind of ugly: poverty and pollution set up against brutish engineering, grim landscapes in grim light. But size, and fear, make both of them sublime—sublime in photographs at least. The sublime is "the most typical of all aesthetic moods," Terry Eagleton writes in *The Ideology of the Aesthetic*, "allowing us as it does to contemplate hostile objects with absolute equanimity." Do people who frequent the megalophobia subreddit actually feel afraid, I wonder, or do they, like me, get pleasure from those photos, "serene in the knowledge" that the objects can't harm us? They're shrunk, behind glass.

I've been thinking about scale because I've been thinking about climate change—or global warming, to be less euphemistic, as the writer-philosopher Timothy Morton advises:

> *Climate change* as a *substitute* for *global warming* is like "cultural change" as a substitute for *Renaissance,* or "change in living conditions" as a substitute for *Holocaust. Climate change* as substitute enables cynical reason (both right wing and left) to say that the "climate has always been changing," which to my ears sounds like using "people have always been killing one another" as a fatuous reason not to control the sale of machine guns.

Morton calls global warming a "hyperobject," something that is "massively distributed in time and space relative to humans." Such objects are more giant than the giant objects of megalophobia; they can't be captured in a photograph or even an abstraction. Time-lapse gifs of melting ice don't help; their extreme compression only minimizes the impact of what's happening at actual size. Global warming is happening everywhere all the time, which paradoxically makes it harder to see, compared to something with defined edges. This is part of the reason we have failed to stop it or even slow it down. How do you fight something you can't comprehend?

The nebulousness of global warming works in the status quo's favor. We don't know exactly how it will play out, which allows fossil-fuel corporations and politicians to exploit that uncertainty, telling the public the facts aren't all in yet—as if doing nothing were the wiser, more cautious move. As with calling it climate change, the call to inaction affects how everyone thinks about global warming. Even those who recognize its urgency can be lulled by its uncertain specific effects, "postponing doom into some hypothetical future," as Morton writes. The disaster seems always just over the horizon. But "the hyperobject spells doom now, not at some future date."

I had forgotten—or maybe never fully understood, or maybe learned and then gone into denial about—the time-delay component of global warming until I read an essay by Chad Harbach, originally published in *n+1* in 2006, which describes this lag:

> It takes forty years or more for the climate to react to the carbon dioxide and methane we emit. This means that the disasters that have already happened during the warmest decade in civilized history (severe droughts in the Sahel region of Africa, Western Australia, and Iberia; deadly flooding in Mumbai; hurricane seasons of unprecedented length, strength, and damage; extinction of many species; runaway glacial melt; deadly heat waves; hundreds of thousands of deaths all told) are not due to our current rates of consumption, but rather the delayed consequences of fuels burned and forests clear-cut decades ago, long before the invention of the Hummer. If we ceased all emissions immediately, global temperatures would continue to rise until around 2050.

I was shocked by this, the idea that the "megadisasters" of 2017 were set into motion in the 1970s, when there were only about half as many humans on Earth.

Even if we did or could stop all carbon emissions now, there's the question of where the existing carbon goes. If we don't invent and implement some kind of technology that removes carbon from the atmosphere (aka "negative emissions"), it will take natural processes tens or possibly hundreds of thousands of years to renormalize—to return to a state that's normal, that is, for us. Take as an example the Paleocene-Eocene Thermal Maximum, 55.5 million years ago, when an enormous amount of carbon and methane were suddenly released into the atmosphere, for reasons that remain unclear. This is the closest known analogue in Earth's history to modern-day global warming. It caused a warm period during which average temperatures increased by five to eight degrees Celsius. Fossil records show that, at the time, the poles resembled the Florida Everglades, hosting crocodiles instead of polar bears. There was no surface ice. This warm period lasted about 200,000 years and was actually a boon for the evolution of mammals and specifically primates; without it, we might not exist.

Morton calls the time scales involved in global warming alternately "horrifying," "terrifying," "petrifying," and "truly humiliating." It is easier to imagine infinity, he says, than very large finitudes: "For every object in the universe there is a genuinely *future future* that is radically unknowable." Nuclear waste, another example of a hyperobject, similarly forces us to contemplate the deep future. Plutonium-239, which is used in both nuclear weapons and reactors, has a half-life of 24,110 years. (The specificity is almost comical, but nuclear materials are exact about when they decay; they're essentially atomic clocks.)

It's hard to know—and easier not to think about—the effects that all the nuclear materials on the planet could have on people, other organisms, and the environment over the course of hundreds of thousands of years. This kind of time-delayed destruction is what the writer Rob Nixon calls "slow violence," a violence "that occurs gradually and out of sight . . . dispersed across time and space." Nixon's book *Slow Violence and the Environmentalism of the Poor* explores how processes like toxic drift, global distillation (also known as the grasshopper effect, which causes pollutants to accrue at the poles), and the acidification of the oceans unfold so slowly they "can hinder our efforts to mobilize and act decisively." The emphasis here is on action—not the object per se but the work it does. An idea as large and amorphous as global warming blurs the distinction between object and process: To look at the moving object we have to pause it, which renders it inert, allowing us to contemplate it passively.

Nixon shows how poor communities and the global South are forced to bear the brunt of "long dyings." He quotes a leaked memo from 1991 signed by Lawrence Summers, then president of the World Bank: "I've always thought that countries in Africa are vastly under polluted . . . Just between you and me, shouldn't the World

Bank be encouraging more migration of the dirty industries to the Least Developed Countries?" We in the "developed world" can ignore slow violence because so much
of it takes place in the far future and the far elsewhere, not
here and not to us.

One way to minimize the apparent damage of globaliza-
tion and capitalism is by setting arbitrary time limits on the
effects of our actions. We can say, for example, how many
people we killed during the years we occupied Vietnam,
without including the "hundreds of thousands [who] survived the official war years, only to slowly lose their lives later
to Agent Orange," Nixon writes. The toxic herbicide continues to build up in food sources like fish; it's linked to birth
defects and Parkinson's disease. Paul Virilio called the Gulf
War "a local war of small interest," but it was also the first
to make use of depleted uranium in warfare, which has,
Nixon writes, "a durability beyond our comprehension," a
half-life of over 4.5 billion years: "When it enters the environment," he writes, depleted uranium "effectively does so
for all time."

The effects of depleted uranium are disputed, but an
army nurse named Carol Picou who worked on the so-
called Highway of Death in Kuwait, a strip of road filled
with wrecked and abandoned vehicles and other debris
from an airborne attack, showed signs of what sounds like
radiation poisoning:

Within days of her departure from the scene, Picou's skin
started to erupt in black spots; soon she lost control of

her bladder and her bowels . . . Over the months and years that followed, she developed thyroid problems and squamous cancer cells in her uterus; she developed immunological dysfunction and encephalopathy. Three years after her stint on the Highway of Death, tests found dangerously elevated levels of uranium in her urine.

In 1996, the Department of Defense discharged Picou, but the documentation calls her condition "non-combat-related": "Etiology Unknown." Nixon writes, "She was thus denied the kind of pension that servicewomen and men injured in the battlefield secured." Picou became one of the *hibakusha* of the world, the often unacknowledged victims of nuclear weapons and disaster. More than 250,000 U.S. veterans of the Gulf War (out of about 700,000 total) complain of continuing health problems, a mysterious chronic illness known as Gulf War Syndrome. But like many conditions we don't understand, the syndrome is often written off as, essentially, hysteria. In *Hystories*, Elaine Showalter argued that Gulf War Syndrome was a psychogenic disorder, like a fear we can catch from the internet just by learning it exists.

The media does spread "infectious" ideas—sensational reporting has been shown to lead to clusters of suicides and spikes in mass shootings. But that explanation often masks human error or, worse, willful obfuscation. As Nixon notes, for decades the military dismissed the health crisis caused by Agent Orange as "a grand hallucination."

Slow violence, according to Nixon, is "underrepresented in strategic planning as well as in human memory." If we can't see it, we can't remember it, nor can we really imagine its future. As the journalist Susan D. Moeller notes in her book *Compassion Fatigue: How the Media Sell Disease, Famine, War and Death*, the media and memory are both highly visual. Spectacular disasters like earthquakes, hurricanes, and floods are newsworthy, but climate change is not. You can package the symptoms, but not the disease.

Both Moeller and Nixon are concerned that we can't properly react to or prepare for less visible disasters until we modify our methods of storytelling: We must find a way to turn them into "arresting stories" (in Nixon's terms), told "in a distinctive manner" (in Moeller's)—suggesting that the right response to unending wars and a rapidly warming planet is a shift in aesthetics. Perhaps it is. Perhaps we have to make the real threats *fascinating*. But how, if we lack the cognitive capacity to see them?

One of the defining properties of hyperobjects is "nonlocality"—they are here and not here; their massive scale deceives the mind. Morton refers to a passage in William Wordsworth's long poem *The Prelude*, in which the poet recalls rowing a boat, at first in peace and then with dread, under a "craggy ridge" that appears at first "an elfin pinnace" but seems to grow and even chase him as he rows away. This impression is due, Morton writes, "to a strange parallax effect in which more of a suitably massive object is revealed as one goes farther away from it." Similarly, I have noticed that airplanes look much larger from a medium distance—when the plane is taxiing on a bridge over the highway as you drive toward the airport, say—than close up, when you're sitting at the gate or boarding the plane. The hyperobject is evasive, always partly hidden.

The cover of *Hyperobjects* offers an impossible view. It's an iceberg shaped like Africa, the exposed part sparkling in sunrays, but you can see the whole thing from top to bottom, both above and below the water—a cross section of reality, like a science museum diorama by Thomas Kinkaid. It reminded me of something—the title, the shade of blue, the sense of something floating—but it took me a few days to figure out what. It was *Hyperspace*, by the physicist Michio Kaku, published almost twenty years earlier. I remember seeing my older brother read it when I was in high school, its paperback cover showing a vaguely surrealist cube hovering over a field with blue sky behind it.

Hyperspace is in part an exercise in conceptualizing spatial dimensions beyond the usual three. As Kaku explains, "The growing realization among scientists today is that any three-dimensional theory is 'too small' to describe the forces that govern our universe." Extra dimensions give us "'enough room' to explain the fundamental forces." Again, later, he writes, "In higher dimensions, knots are easily unraveled and rings can be intertwined. This is because there is 'more room' in which to move ropes past each other and rings into each other."

The word "room" makes me think of *a* room, an empty cube. But higher dimensions, like the abyss of deep time, are difficult, if not impossible, to imagine. Kaku writes that "even experienced mathematicians and theoretical physicists who have worked with higher-dimensional spaces for years admit that they cannot visualize them." However, there are techniques designed to make it easier. The mathematician Charles Hinton, while working at Oxford in the late 1800s, devised a series of tricks intended to help people "see" four-dimensional objects.

The most well-known of these thought experiments involves a "hypercube," a four-dimensional cube. You can unfold the sides of a regular cube into a two-dimensional object, six squares lying flat in the shape of a cross. A two-dimensional being could perceive the cross of squares but could only imagine what the higher-dimensional, folded-up cube might look like. Analogously, Hinton proposed, a hypercube can be "unfolded" into a three-dimensional object—he called this a "tesseract"—which looks like a cross made of eight cubes. You can see an example in Salvador Dalí's painting *Corpus Hypercubus*, in which Jesus is crucified on a tesseract. The exercise is to try to imagine what the tesseract would look like "folded" back up into its real shape.

There's something misleading about these exercises, though, as well as the idea of higher dimensions creating "more room"—they make it seem like the fourth and fifth dimensions, and so on, are larger somehow, more outside. But where? As high up or far down as you can imagine is still in the third dimension. But counterintuitively, some theoretical physicists think higher dimensions are smaller, not bigger, than the ones we perceive. The physicist Peter Freund says we can't see them because they are "'curled up' into a tiny ball so small that they can no longer be detected." These curled-up dimensions are on the scale of the "Planck length," a unit 100 billion billion times smaller than a proton. Of course, to a normal brain this makes as little sense as trying to imagine the extra dimensions "outside" our three dimensions. How do you escape the third dimension by going farther inside? What order of dimension you're in is somewhat academic when the scale itself is inconceivable.

Kaku, writing in 1996, reported that physicists speculate that hyperspace—entailing, as it does, wormholes, or portals into other parts of space-time or even other universes—could save us somehow from the fiery end of the universe, a reversal of the Big Bang known as the Big Crunch, when "all life forms will be crushed beyond recognition." "Scientists and philosophers, like Charles Darwin and Bertrand Russell," Kaku writes, "have written mournfully about the futility of our pitiful existence, knowing that our civilization will inexorably die when our world ends"—unless hyperspace provides an escape hatch.

Now this idea sounds a little quaint. Recent evidence suggests there will be no Big Crunch, because the expansion of the universe appears to be accelerating. If it keeps doing that "forever," the death of the universe will be "cold." Objects will get farther and farther apart until the universe reaches a state of maximum entropy, when nothing else can happen. But either way, the end is the end, most likely many trillions of years from now—in what sense would the "us" that makes it there be "us"? More to the point, I can't imagine a scientist or philosopher in the twenty-first century worrying about the eventual fate of the greater universe. A different kind of heat death—global warming—is a far more imminent existential threat.

A progress trap is a development that looks at first like a clear advancement but in time proves to actually de-optimize the system. The classic example is the invention of weapons, which helped early humans become much more efficient at hunting but then led to the extinction of megafauna. According to Ronald Wright, who wrote a book about these traps called A *Short History of Progress*, the problem is often one of scale: Trying to scale up technologies that work on the local level leads to depletion of resources and other unforeseen consequences that can ultimately collapse the system.

It may be that civilization itself is a progress trap. A theory known as "the Great Filter" proposes that the reason we haven't found compelling evidence of advanced civilizations elsewhere in the universe is that there aren't any, at least not any advanced enough that they could reach us. There may be a "filter" somewhere in the evolution of life that puts a ceiling on advancement—for example, maybe any civilization sufficiently advanced to develop deep space travel will quickly exhaust the energy needed to sustain it. Or maybe it will inadvertently destroy itself through nuclear warfare or a runaway artificial intelligence.

"Since World War II, the sum total of scientific knowledge has doubled every 10 to 20 or so years," Kaku writes, "so the progress of science and technology into the twenty-first century may surpass our wildest expectations." When I was in college, I read Ray Kurzweil's *The Age of Spiritual Machines* and completely accepted its techno-optimism; Kurzweil believed that "the singularity," a tipping point after which technology would advance so rapidly that we couldn't possibly predict or imagine what developments would be possible, was upon us. For years I told people we might be the last generation to die, or we might not die at all but be "uploaded" out of our bodies so that we could theoretically live on eternally, as data. To be clear, I have lost all faith in this theory. I no longer assume that technology will save us.

The economist Leopold Kohr believed most social dysfunction was the result of "the cult of bigness," the unexamined assumption that growth is always good. In *The Overdeveloped Nations: The Diseconomies of Scale*, Kohr recounts an incident in New York City, a man threatening suicide from a high window. The first bystanders were "terror-struck," but as the crowd grew, "the pangs of individual conscience were insensibly drowned in the throb of socialized excitement." They turned mean and taunting; someone called to the man to "make it snappy." When the crowd dispersed, the few who stayed went back to praying

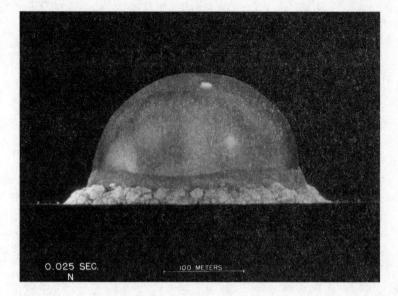

0.025 SEC.
N
| 100 METERS |

for the suicidal man. "This had nothing to do with their
better selves," according to Kohr, but the return of the
group to a "sub-critical mass"—"the tenuous translucency
of which makes it impossible for an individual to hide his
action from his own conscience." A crowded world, then,
has a dangerous opacity, providing cover for cruelty and
corruption.

In *Hyperobjects*, Morton claims that "the end of the
world has already occurred"—more than once, in fact,
since "for something to happen it often needs to happen
twice." It ended first in 1784, with the invention of the
steam engine, and again in 1945, when we tested the first
atomic bomb—two events commonly named as the starting

point of the Anthropocene. He includes a photograph of the Trinity test at 0.016 seconds, a horrifying membrane-bubble like an alien jellyfish the size of a town. The photo was originally banned, "since it was considered far more provocative than the habitual mushroom cloud." Unlike a cloud, the bubble did not look natural.

This reminds me of the Buddhist philosophy known as "broken glass practice": Don't be upset when a teacup breaks, because its breaking was inevitable; therefore, it was already broken. Is the world already broken? I wonder if humanity is not "too big to fail," but too big not to.

2018

THE GREAT MORTALITY

One day in April, I filled a glass with tap water from our kitchen sink and noticed that it tasted unusually good—a bit creamy somehow, a bit savory in the manner of club soda, which is superior to seltzer because of the sodium. It seemed especially thirst-quenching, yet so tasty I kept drinking more of it. A brewer I know told me Colorado water has more mineral content in the spring months due to mountain runoff, which might explain the change in flavor. I loved that idea.

But the explanation didn't hold up. My husband, John, thought our water tasted the same as ever. More strikingly, every liquid I drank started to taste better to me. Wines tasted richer and more buttery; cheap wines tasted like they'd been aged for years in oak. Bourbon tasted sweeter and creamier too, almost like coconut. Canned seltzer tasted especially great, like an indulgence instead of a substitute. This went on for weeks. The internet told me I might be pregnant or diabetic. I was quite sure neither was true. Instead, I grew increasingly suspicious that I might have a brain tumor.

I mentioned the symptom to my brother in a text: "I think I have brain cancer? My palate suddenly changed." He responded right away: "I had that! It was a virus. Everything tasted weird and I couldn't handle spicy food at all. It lasted a few weeks." It didn't sound like what I had, but I was heartened nonetheless. But if it was a virus, why didn't anyone else have it? I mentioned it to everyone I saw, hoping for a sign of recognition. "It's not unpleasant," I'd always say.

Finally, about three weeks in, John and I were reading on the couch; he took a sip of water and literally smacked his lips. "Mmm," he said. "That tastes delicious." "Oh my god!" I grabbed his arm. "You have the virus!" John's virus, if it was a virus, didn't last as long, or maybe he just wasn't as attuned to it as I was. In any case, it went away, for both of us. Boxed wine tasted cheap again.

Years ago, when I was in grad school, I saw the philosopher Daniel Dennett deliver a lecture about memes—memes in the Richard Dawkins sense ("a unit of cultural transmission"). Dennett talked about a kind of parasite, the *Dicrocoelium dendriticum*, or lancet liver fluke, that infects ants; it makes them "want" to crawl to the tops of tall blades of grass. (What does desire feel like to an ant?) But that is not the end goal for the parasite. Those ants high up in the grass are more likely to be eaten by grazing cows, and that's what the parasite "wants." This mechanism is called parasitic mind control: The fluke wants to be inside the cow; it thrives in the guts of the cow and then gets the reproductive benefit of being shit out into the pasture, where it can infect more ants.

Both parasites and microparasites (viruses and bacteria) can hijack our minds; they make us act weird. *Toxoplasma gondii*, a parasite found in cat feces, makes mice less afraid of cats; this is an evolutionary strategy, making it easier for the parasite to get from the mouse to the cat. It can spread to people too, where it may increase risk-taking in general. One bizarre study found that people, presumably cat owners, with toxoplasmosis "are more likely to major in business." An NBC News story suggested optimistically that the parasite "may give people the courage they need to become entrepreneurs."

If true (and I doubt it), that would be an extreme case of a microscopic parasite altering the course of your whole life. But ordinary viruses change our behavior too. A 2010 study found that people became more sociable in the forty-eight hours after they were exposed to the flu virus, the period when they are contagious but not symptomatic. The infected hosts, researchers noted, were significantly "more likely to head out to bars and parties." Even symptoms we think of as purely physical reflexes can be construed as behavior changes. In *Guns, Germs, and Steel,* Jared Diamond writes that "many of our 'symptoms' of disease actually represent ways in which some damned clever microbe modifies our bodies or our behavior such that we become enlisted to spread microbes." The tuberculosis bacterium, for example, makes us want to cough, atomizing it into breathable air. According to the Mayo Clinic, this can happen when a tubercular patient "coughs, speaks, sneezes, spits, laughs or sings." This makes me wonder if consumption ever makes patients giggly, or more likely to burst into song, despite the chest pain and malaise. A disease called kuru can cause what are often described as "pathological bursts of laughter." It is not, however, spread by laughing. It was common among the Fore tribe in Papua New Guinea until the cause was discovered to be prions, spread by the practice of funerary cannibalism—eating your dead.

One of the creepiest behavioral changes caused by a virus is hydrophobia, a symptom of "classic encephalitic rabies," also known as "furious rabies." It's not an exaggeration: People and animals infected with rabies become morbidly terrified of water. Or perhaps more accurately, they're of two minds about water—they both want it and can't stand the thought or sight of it. (It's the opposite of my virus, then, which made beverages extra appealing.) Here's how Bill Wasik and Monica Murphy describe it in their book *Rabid: A Cultural History of the World's Most Diabolical Virus*: "Present the hydrophobic patient with a cup of water and, desperately though he wants to drink it, his entire body rebels against the consummation of this act. The outstretched arm jerks away just as it is about to bring the cup to the parched lips. Other times the entire body convulses at the thought."

Why does this happen? It's not so you'll die of thirst. The virus's goal is not to kill you—though it does do that;

once symptoms appear, close to 100 percent of rabies patients die—but to spread. The "sole mission" of a virus, according to Connie Goldsmith, the author of *Pandemic: How Climate, the Environment, and Superbugs Increase the Risk,* "is to get inside a cell and turn it into a factory to produce new viruses." Viruses, unlike bacteria and parasites, are not even alive, yet they, too, have desires.

The rabies virus takes up in the animal's spit. According to an article in the *Merck Manual of Diagnosis and Therapy*:

> Most people become restless, confused, and uncontrollably excited. Their behavior may be bizarre. They may hallucinate and have insomnia. Saliva production greatly increases. Spasms of the muscles in the throat and larynx occur because rabies affects the area in the brain that controls swallowing, speaking, and breathing. The spasms can be excruciatingly painful. A slight breeze or an attempt to drink water can trigger the spasms. Thus, people with rabies cannot drink.

The spread of the virus to the salivary glands explains the telltale foaming at the mouth in rabid dogs, and the spread to the brain explains their rage, which drives them to attack and bite. This rabid madness, and its transmission through biting, gave birth to mythological monsters from zombies to werewolves and vampires. The association of vampires with bats stems from their acting as a "reservoir host" for rabies—bats can carry the virus without dying from it.

Rabies—like malaria, Zika, typhus, bubonic plague, and all flus—is a zoonosis, a disease that makes the leap from animal to human. That leap, the transmission, is called spillover. In his book *Ebola: The Natural and Human History of a Deadly Virus*, David Quammen describes "zoonosis" as "a word of the future"—"destined for heavy use in the 21st century." Dangerous infectious diseases persist only when they have a reservoir host. We were able to eradicate smallpox, Quammen notes, because it's *not* a zoonosis; it only infects humans, and once we've cured them all, it has nowhere else to hide.

The reservoir host for Ebola is still not known. It was initially spread to humans when hungry villagers in Africa ate infected apes, but apes are not an unharmed, oblivious reservoir—where there are outbreaks of Ebola in humans, there are also dead gorillas. It seems likely that, as with the lyssaviruses that cause rabies, the host is some kind of bat. When Quammen went hunting for reservoirs in Bangladesh, the epidemiologist Jonathan Epstein told him, "Keep your mouth closed when you look up." You don't want an Ebola bat flying overhead to shit in your mouth.

During the 1950s and '60s, there was great optimism that the world would soon be rid of all deadly infectious disease. The United States spent huge sums of money on a campaign to eliminate malaria in the so-called Third World—an act of charity, in a way, since malaria was not a threat in affluent countries. The plan not only failed—perhaps we gave up too soon, or perhaps it was an impossible task—but actually made the problem worse. The campaign reduced local immunity to malaria, while the virus evolved resistance to known treatments such as chloroquine. At the same time, heavy use of pesticides killed off many beneficial insects while the mosquitoes became resistant to the chemicals. As Laurie Garrett puts it in *The Coming Plague: Newly Emerging Diseases in a World Out of Balance*, "Almost overnight resistant mosquito populations appeared all over the world." Rachel Carson, the author of *Silent Spring*, said at the time, "The insect enemy has been made stronger by our efforts." After seeming to die down, cases of malaria resurged, now in a new, iatrogenic form—"created as a result of medical treatment," Garrett writes.

Malaria had become something strange and ill-defined. "What *is* malaria?" Kent Campbell, a doctor with the Centers for Disease Control, has asked. In many parts of Africa, it's endemic and omnipresent but often asymptomatic. Previously, children with malaria either died or became largely immune. Now children might survive but lapse into fatal anemia years later, requiring blood transfusions—not ideal when AIDS is epidemic too. Further complicating matters, when a child in Africa has a fever, it's standard procedure to give the child antimalarials, but just because a child has malarial parasites does not necessarily mean that any given fever is caused by malaria. In this way, it's like climate change: Every bad storm feels as though it must be related to global warming, but you can't say with complete certainty that any given storm is the direct result of climate change. And, as Campbell says, "we cannot continue to treat every fever as if it's malaria, because the roster of drugs is getting shorter." Yet a malarial fever can lead to death, and malaria is still a top-ten cause of death in low-income countries.

To answer his own question about the nature of malaria, Campbell eventually concluded that "malaria is a disease that responds to antimalarial drugs." He did not name a specific drug, since the drugs have to change. It made me think of a conversation I had years ago with an ex-boyfriend, a physics major, who told me that temperature is not as simple a concept as it seems. It is not synonymous with heat or energy, he said. Temperature, essentially, is what thermometers measure. I never really understood this, but I think about it often. Or maybe I should say, what I think about is the elegant way the construction reduces what we understand.

There's a social media phenomenon I've started calling the performative death wish. I noticed it recently when archaeologists found an unopened black sarcophagus in Alexandria. Some feared that the tomb might contain a deadly virus or bacteria or just a curse—after King Tut's tomb was opened, in 1922, a number of people associated with the excavation died. "I'm pinning all my hopes on the creature in the sarcophagus," one woman tweeted. Another tweet went:

2012: oh no Mayan calendar says the world might end and
we could all die

2018: PLEASE let the black Egyptian sarcophagus carry a
curse that will collectively put us out of our misery

Whenever a story on the threat of an "extinction-level event," like an asteroid or a comet headed for Earth, is making the rounds, people quote-tweet it to add, "Finally, some good news!"

In this age of horrible news all the time, we understand it instantly: ironic suicidal ideation. But there's something real behind it—the fantasy of the swift death, the instinct to just get it over with. Of course, the asteroid that killed the dinosaurs didn't kill them instantly, unless they were at ground zero. It wasn't "IPU annihilation," to use the philosopher Galen Strawson's term: instant, painless, unexperienced. It took tens of thousands, possibly even hundreds of thousands, of years of living on a sick and barren planet before they all finally went extinct. This makes the prospect of death by asteroid much less merciful.

Death may represent a kind of escape, but is this posturing really about wanting to escape, or is it about wanting to *suffer*? Lately, when I luck into an excellent bag of cherries or an especially luscious peach, I think, automatically: *I don't deserve this.* When people say they're quitting social media because it doesn't make them happy, I think, *Wrong reason.* I think, *We don't deserve to be happy.* It feels related to the death wish, my own version of liberal guilt run amok, transformed into a longing for punishment.

During the Black Death in Europe, bands of flagellants would roam from town to town, like a traveling theater troupe, putting on public performances of violent self-punishment. They would flog themselves with leather-and-iron whips while crying out to God, "Spare us!" As the historian Barbara Tuchman writes in A *Distant Mirror*, "The flagellants saw themselves as redeemers who, by re-enacting the scourging of Christ upon their own bodies and making the blood flow, would atone for human wickedness and earn another chance for mankind." In the absence of a better explanation, medieval people blamed themselves for the disease: "Hardly an act or thought, sexual, mercantile or military, did not contravene the dictates of the Church . . . The result was an underground lake of guilt in the soul that the plague now tapped." But the flagellants didn't take all the blame; they also scapegoated the Jews, accusing them of poisoning wells. In Basel in 1349, Tuchman writes, "the whole community of several hundred Jews was burned in a wooden house especially constructed for the purpose"—a medieval concentration camp.

Centuries later, we still have a tendency to interpret epidemics as punishment, divine or otherwise. When AIDS emerged in the early 1980s, it was seen as a natural and necessary corrective to gay liberation. People called it "the gay plague." The televangelist Jerry Falwell said, "AIDS is not just God's punishment for homosexuals; it is God's punishment for the society that tolerates homosexuals." Senator Jesse Helms thought people with AIDS brought it on themselves through their "deliberate, disgusting, revolting conduct." As Susan Sontag noted in *AIDS and Its Metaphors*, AIDS, in the United States at least, "is understood as a disease not only of sexual excess but of perversity," which makes it easy to view infection as retribution.

When we don't understand the cause of a disease or how to treat it, we resort to magical thinking. Ebola was initially blamed on sorcery or *ezanga*, a Bakola word meaning "some sort of vampirism or evil spirit," as Quammen writes: "*Ezanga* could even be summoned and targeted at a victim, like casting a hex." But the sorcery explanation fell apart the more the illness spread: "Sorcery does not kill without reason, does not kill everybody, and does not kill gorillas," one Mbomo woman said—even sorcery has its logic. The apparent senselessness of a new epidemic makes it even more frightening, so that every plague is a double plague of contagion and fear. "The mystery of the contagion was 'the most terrible of all the terrors,'" Tuchman writes of the Black Death, quoting a Flemish cleric. "Ignorance of the cause augmented the sense of horror." Guy de Chauliac, a doctor who treated three popes in succession, wrote that he lived in "continual fear." (Why is it so hard for me to imagine their fear? The centuries have a neutralizing effect; I imagine they accepted what they called "the great mortality" as a fact of history in the same way I do.)

The best medical science at the time of the Black Death

almost came close to an approximate understanding of how the plague spread. "That the infection came from contact was quickly observed but not comprehended," Tuchman writes. Some thought it was transferred by sight—the evil eye. This is why plague masks had crystal eyepieces in addition to beaks stuffed with aromatics, to protect the wearer against both malevolent glances and miasma, the foul air that was really the stink of death. One physician determined that infection was "communicated by means of air breathed in and out"—which was true. The plague took several forms and could be spread through blood-to-blood contact, like hepatitis, or through coughing, like tuberculosis or the flu. (Garrett notes that "conditions in European cities of the fifteenth to the seventeenth century were ideal for transmission of *M. tuberculin*, especially during the winter, when the practice was to shut all windows and huddle around a heat source"—death by coziness.) But since no one knew what germs were, the doctor "had to assume the air was corrupted by planetary influences." In 1348, the medical faculty of the University of Paris delivered a report on the cause of the pestilence: "a triple conjunction of Saturn, Jupiter, and Mars in the 40th degree of Aquarius." As late as 1918, physicians named "cosmic influence" as a factor in the mysteriously deadly Spanish flu—"influence" and "influenza" have the same etymology, a "flowing in," as of unseen, ethereal forces.

If the plague had been sent to punish people for their sins—Matteo Villani, a fourteenth-century historian, compared it to the great flood "in ultimate purpose"—you might think that the period following the plague years would be one of great austerity. If anything, the opposite is the case. Survivors of the plague did not become ascetic. Instead, they may have sensed a baffling meaninglessness to their being spared—survivor's guilt being a kind of miserable apprehension of one's own good luck. "If the purpose had been to shake man from his sinful ways," Tuchman writes, "it had failed." People embraced "a more disordered and shameful life," and "behavior grew more reckless and callous, as it often does after a period of violence and suffering." You could also say not much had changed at all, though a third of the world had died: "What was the human condition after the plague? Exhausted by deaths and sorrows and the morbid excesses of fear and hate, it ought to have shown some profound effects, but no radical change was immediately visible. The persistence of the normal is strong."

Or, as William H. McNeill writes in *Plagues and Peoples*, the plague on some level was "a routine crisis of human life." Many at the time seemed to take this mass die-off in stride, "like the weather." It's paradoxical, how quickly we adapt to suffering.

A *Distant Mirror*, published in 1978, was so named because Tuchman felt that the awfulness of the fourteenth century— for years, she says, historians tended "to skirt the century because it could not be made to fit into a pattern of human progress"—had clear parallels in the awfulness of the twentieth century. (In my notes, I wrote, *You thought that was bad?* then crossed it out many times.) Her follow-up, in 1984, was *The March of Folly*, which explores why people and particularly governments frequently act against their own interests: "Why do holders of high office so often act contrary to the way reason points and enlightened self-interest suggests?" Why, for example, "does American business insist on 'growth' when it is demonstrably using up the three basics of life on our planet—land, water, and unpolluted air?" Our inaction in the face of global warming seems a clear case of this. And we've had forty years to get our shit together. As a recent *New York Times* feature noted, "Nearly everything we understand about global warming was understood in 1979." Why can't we or won't we save ourselves?

A few weeks ago, John handed me a book he must have seen on the new books shelf at our library. It was *Pandemic*, by Connie Goldsmith. Relevant to my interests, certainly, but, I pointed out to him, "This is a children's book." More accurately, it's young adult nonfiction, probably intended as a middle school textbook. I tossed it on my giant pile of plague books and assumed I wouldn't get to it. As it happens, it was the last book I read in my research for this essay, and I found it surprisingly good and helpful. Goldsmith lays out how five global trends—climate change, disruption of animal habitats, increased air travel, crowding and megacities, and overuse and misuse of antibiotics—all increase the risk of a pandemic.

"Pandemic" sounds to me like automatic hyperbole, like "pandemonium," but it's a fairly well-defined term in epidemiology: Unlike an "outbreak," which affects limited people in a limited area for a short time, or an "epidemic," which affects a larger number of people in multiple areas at the same time, "pandemics affect many people in many parts of the world at the same time." The Black Death might have been the most pandemic of pandemics, but we could point to the Spanish flu as a more recent example, and HIV could qualify as well. In Western countries, we almost think of AIDS as a solved problem, since antiviral treatments have dramatically improved both quality of life and life span for people infected with HIV. But about half the people who have contracted the virus in history have died from it, making it as deadly as Ebola, and its transmission is far from contained in Africa.

All five of Goldsmith's global risk factors are, in essence, our fault: "Scientists do not yet know what will cause the next pandemic. It could be a new bacterium that resists all available medications. Or it could be a mutated virus to which people have no immunity. What scientists and epidemiologists do know is that human activity is largely responsible for the spread of disease." No wonder new and reemerging diseases feel like punishment. Mosquitoes and other "vectors" (usually biting and stinging insects that help carry diseases between humans and other animal hosts), for example, are getting a leg up from global warming. They like warm, wet environments, so as temperatures rise and flooding increases, their territory expands. More monstrously, "hotter temperatures make mosquitos hungrier," and "warm air incubates the virus faster."

Relatedly, ticks have become more of a problem, in part due to suburban development in wooded areas where ticks live. In the United States, Lyme disease is now the most common vector-borne illness as well as one of the fastest-growing infectious diseases. And it is not well understood; there is disagreement over whether chronic Lyme disease even exists. But many patients continue to experience symptoms after treatment. This could be due to persistent bacteria not killed by antibiotics, or to permanent immune damage that causes your body to respond to the infection even after it's gone, like phantom pain. Goldsmith quotes the epidemiologist Ali S. Khan: "We humans act like we own the planet, when really it's the microbes and the insects that run things. One way they remind us who's in charge is by transmitting disease, often with the help of small animals, including rodents and bats." This is zoonosis as revenge, by the animal kingdom or Mother Nature writ large.

Back in 1981, the toxicologist Mark Lappé wrote a book titled *Germs That Won't Die*, warning of the microbe mutations he saw happening in hospitals. "We have organisms now proliferating that never existed before in nature," he wrote. "We have changed the whole face of the earth by the use of antibiotics"—the medical Anthropocene. Critics at the time felt Lappé was grossly overstating the problem. Now so-called superbugs, or antibiotic-resistant bacterial strains like MRSA, kill about 700,000 people in the world every year, similar to the number killed by mosquitoes, the deadliest animal by some margin, deadlier even than humans.

Antibiotic resistance is often blamed on people not taking their medications correctly, but it's not that simple. Only 20 percent of antibiotics in the United States are used on people; the rest are for animals. Often these are the same antibiotics that humans take. Bacteria in animals then develop resistance to those antibiotics, and when they infect humans, the drugs don't work for us. Worrisomely, new antibiotics are not an exploding area of medical research; we've had fewer new ones every decade since the 1980s, and most are just variations of existing drugs, which are unlikely to remain effective against already resistant bacteria for long. Goldsmith suggests that the bulk of pharmaceutical R&D budgets may go to long-term maintenance medications rather than those used to cure one-time infections, since the former are more profitable over time.

Many experts think the most likely culprit of a future pandemic is some version of the flu; flus are common, highly contagious, and especially dangerous when there's a new strain to which people have limited immunity. There is hope that another pandemic on the level of the Spanish flu might be avoided through the development of a universal flu vaccine, which could be made possible with enough resources and support. But, to state the obvious, vaccines only work when we take them.

In *Rabid*, Wasik and Murphy note that "immediately upon the creation" of the smallpox vaccine in 1796, there were "scientists and laypeople" who believed the vaccine was "poison." In other words, antivaxxers are as old as vaccines. Twentieth-century advances like the polio vaccine strengthened public support. "For two decades," in the 1950s and '60s, Garrett writes in *The Coming Plague*, "insurance carriers, politicians, drug companies, and the judicial system adhered to the basic principle that the rights of an immunized society superseded those of small numbers of individuals." But a scare in 1976, when recipients of a new swine flu vaccine seemed to have higher than average incidence of Guillain-Barré syndrome, caused permanent PR damage. Guillain-Barré, which can lead to (usually reversible) paralysis and other neurological symptoms that require hospitalization, can occur after any infectious disease, including the flu. The ensuing panic would "haunt all vaccine efforts inside the United States for decades," Garrett writes, though the increased risk was very small: "approximately one additional case of GBS for every 100,000 people who got the swine flu vaccine," according to the CDC. Typical flu shots most likely do not increase the risk: "Studies suggest that it is more likely that a person will get GBS after getting the flu than after vaccination."

The antivaccination movement now seems to be in another waxing period—there have been outbreaks of formerly very rare diseases like measles both in the United States and in Europe. We can't blame it on anything other than ignorance. We know the flu vaccine works (I'm tempted to write, *"We" "know" it "works"*), but most people don't know *how* it works. I'm not saying people don't understand how it works on a technical level; we don't even grasp the basics. I've heard intelligent people I know say, "I never got the flu until the one year I got the flu shot. Never again!" People treat the flu shot like a matter of personal choice. They think if they don't get a shot and then they get the flu, that's their own bad luck. But the flu shot, like other vaccines, is truly effective only when taken en masse; it reduces overall infection in a population so that the most vulnerable people—usually the elderly, but for some strains it's children—are less likely to be infected. This is collective, social action—collective inoculation. Further, the folk idea that some years the flu shot "doesn't work" is inaccurate. Flu shots always contain a mix of vaccines against several different strains that are believed most likely to be dominant that flu season. Vaccine makers don't always get it right, but the range of effectiveness is more like 30 to 60 percent; it's not 0 or 100 percent. Even in an off year, the flu shot increases your immunity, and if you do get sick, you'll probably be *less* sick and sick for a shorter time—and therefore less contagious.

The immunologist Anthony Fauci has said that "in some respects, vaccines are the victims of their own success"— meaning that, when used properly, they can almost eliminate incidence of an infectious disease. But then people stop dying of that disease, and it stops seeming like a threat. So we get lax about the "cure"—though often these diseases can't be cured, only prevented. This feels related to the false assumption that World War II cured humanity of fascism forever. By Garrett's account, "every problem seemed conquerable" in the decade after the Allies defeated Hitler. Instead, fascism had just gone quiet for a while, a virus hidden in an unidentified reservoir host. In Siberia recently, long-frozen anthrax emerged from thawing permafrost, killing a bunch of reindeer and some children. What other ancient plagues are in there, preserved cryogenically?

"Folly is a child of power," Tuchman writes—the result of feeling invincible. We make stupid decisions because we think, having come this far (as a culture? as a species?) we're indestructible. On some unexpected level, I almost fear we are. Even if we don't succumb to the worst doomsday scenarios involved in climate change (aka "Hothouse Earth"), the climate is certain to get worse and become less hospitable to humans in the short term. A lot of people, especially near coasts, especially near the equator and in poverty-stricken areas, will be displaced, will suffer, and will die. But some of us will remain, facing a very different reality.

It seems unlikely, when we remember the slow tapering off of the dinosaurs, that we'll all be wiped out in some kind of purifying "clean sweep," that anti-fantasy. (Have we started to think of humanity itself as a plague on the planet? A friend of mine, when I mentioned that male sperm counts have been dropping for decades, basically said, "Good riddance.") There's some evidence that reduced population and reforestation after the Black Death helped trigger a mini ice age; that wasn't any fun for the plague survivors, considering it led to famine. But if there is another "great mortality," it might have a tiny bit of upside in the long view of history: A pandemic, an asteroid, or a nuclear war could all lead to global cooling. It could offset some of our gravest errors and reset the planet.

When you look at it that way, it's almost as though we are acting with a higher collective intelligence—a hive mind, employing folly as a strategy. But perhaps it's too generous to call it intelligence; perhaps it's just a mechanism, like whatever makes the parasite that drives the ant suicidally up the grass blade "want" what it "wants." We don't know what we want, or what purpose we serve.

2018

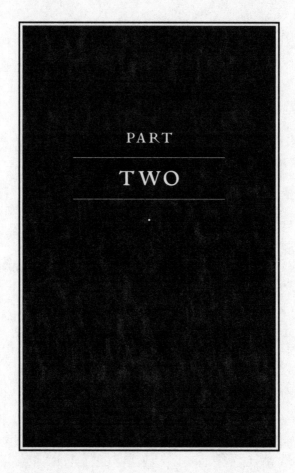

PART

TWO

THE LITTLE ROOM
(OR, THE UNREALITY OF MEMORY)

My maternal grandmother moved into her house, her last house, in 1962. My mother and uncle were twelve and fourteen at the time. It was six years after her first husband died of lung cancer—my mother has said she never saw him without a cigar or cigarette in his hand. (He was my grandfather, but never having met him, I don't think of him that way.) My grandmother lived in this house with her second husband until he died of a fall and a subsequent hemorrhage in 1988, then remained there alone until 2001, when she had a stroke. She survived the stroke, mentally intact, but with partial paralysis on her right side; my parents moved her into an assisted-living facility and sold the house.

The house changed only superficially from my earliest memories until the last time I saw it, when I was in college. It felt preserved, like a museum. There was a front room, in particular, that seemed frozen in time, because no one ever sat in there—the living room, I suppose, but it felt like

a formal sitting room or parlor. The sofa was strictly orna-
mental, a curvaceous affair covered in an uncomfortable,
silvery-blue brocade; there was something called a cigarette
table, a little tripod end table with a drawer for cigarettes,
and a coffee table with a pink marble top. I've seen washed-
out photos of my mother, square photos with a white
border, posing in this room, in her marching-band uni-
form from high school (she played the marimba), and after
her wedding at a nearby church in 1970. The furniture and
the art on the walls, the china displayed in the china cabi-
net, look exactly the same as they did thirty years later.

As kids, my brother and I spent most of our time in
the more comfortable room toward the back that my grandmother called the den. This room, too, rarely changed. There
was a large wooden console with a built-in TV set, which
had an old-fashioned glass candy jar on the corner and,
above it, rows of shelves that must have held the same
books and knickknacks she had originally placed there
in the early '60s—sets of abridged classics, music boxes, a
little ceramic dog, framed sepia photos of my mother and
uncle in their youth. There was also, on another wall, a set
of portraits, drawn in pastels, of their profiles when they
were teenagers. The room had a kind of extension with
parquet flooring, a green card table, and a closet full of old
games (a cribbage board, dominoes, mahjong, poker chips;
an orange tin labeled PEANUT BRITTLE that contained a
coiled-up "snake" made of fabric covering a spring). Near
the back door was a wrought-iron floor lamp that reminded
me of a streetlight. Next to the closet, there was an alcove

in the wall that held a melodeon, a small antique pump organ that operated with a foot pedal.

If this world was strange and magical to me then, it's even more strange and magical now, for being remote. It's hard for me to believe it no longer exists; it's not a place I can go to. I can see it in such lush and minute detail; I can feel the texture of the scratchy couch cushions and the roughness of the bricks around the fireplace; I can smell the old appliances in the kitchen, the old makeup and face creams in the bathroom vanity. But as rich as the memory is, reproduced to scale like a diorama in my mind, it's not enough, the way it's not enough to know your favorite song by heart and be able to play it note for note in your head—you always need to hear the song again.

Since my grandmother died, a little over a year ago and just before her ninety-fourth birthday, I have often wished I could actually visit the house, the physical house just as I remember it—before we removed what we could keep and sold off the rest in an estate sale. I could walk through the rooms at leisure, and look at the old stuff, the valuables and bric-a-brac, once more. I would bring John with me, to show him all the things that fascinated me as a child and eventually grew familiar. Now it would be a real museum, and we could examine these objects of my childhood—pristine, on exhibit—like they were new again.

"The Mandela Effect" is the theory that a collective false memory is evidence of a crossing or merging of parallel universes. It gets its name from a group of people who "re-member" that Nelson Mandela—the president of South Africa from 1994 to 1999—died in prison in the '80s. (Mandela died at home, from a respiratory infection, in 2013.) What these people are remembering, the theory goes, is the actual past in an alternate reality; somehow they've slipped through and found themselves in our reality with its different but otherwise reconcilable past.

Two examples of the Mandela Effect caused a stir on Reddit within the last several years. In one thread, some people insist that the *Berenstain Bears* series of children's books, written by Stan and Jan Berenstain, was originally named the *Berenstein Bears* (a claim supposedly corroborated by an image of a label on an old VHS tape, most likely bearing a typo). In another, a group of people collectively recall seeing a movie in the '90s called *Shazaam*, starring the comedian Sinbad as a genie. The movie does not exist. Are these people visitors from another stream in the multiverse? More likely, they misremember the spelling of the bear family's name because "-stein" is a more familiar ending for a last name than "-stain," and they misremember the existence of a movie called *Shazaam* because there is, in this world, a movie about a genie, played by Shaquille O'Neal, called *Kazaam* and made in 1996.

If you had seen *Kazaam* once or twice a number of years ago, it's plausible that if a friend mentioned a movie named *Shazaam* to you, starring Sinbad, you could easily picture the cover of the movie—just swap out Shaq for Sinbad. Same pose, same title font. The more you thought about it, the more real it would seem. A false memory can accrue detail over time; we fill in gaps after the fact, perhaps by borrowing from other memories. We don't need to posit an alternate reality to explain the false memories. But for those who "remembered" the Sinbad version, the memory felt entirely real; it seemed to represent and refer to something actual, a verifiable outside thing. In this way, memory itself is an alternate reality—an unreachable place we can somehow *see*.

What happens to collective memory when the referent *is* real and verifiable, a part of our own lived past, is no less mystifying. We can guess what gives rise to conspiracy theories like the belief that the moon landing was faked—a deep distrust of government and the media. And Holocaust denial is of course politically motivated, an apologist impulse that goes so far as to rewrite or overwrite history. It's hard to believe that the first deniers were sincere, though naturally there would have been an element of true disbelief—how could anyone have committed such horrors? But however established the facts, simply questioning history seems to alter collective perception of history. So we must constantly *re*establish the facts, as when Google recently came under fire for ranking a Holocaust denial site first in the results for the search query "did the Holocaust happen"—a case where a page's popularity certainly shouldn't determine its ranking.

In her book *Frames of Remembrance: The Dynamics of Collective Memory*, the Canadian sociologist Iwona Irwin-Zarecka remembers the case of Ernst Zündel, a German

immigrant who went on trial in Toronto for publishing materials denying the occurrence of the Holocaust. According
to Irwin-Zarecka, the local paper in her town of Kitchener,
Ontario, became "a forum for expressing concerns with
the possible damage to the image of Germans as a whole."
It was not Zündel per se who provoked this worry, she says,
but "the very exposure accorded to Auschwitz, day after
day of the long trial." The Jewish community, too, voiced
objections to all the publicity: "Since the judge decided
then that the historical facticity of the Holocaust would
be argued in court, the deniers were seen as having
won the battle no matter what the verdict. Both sides believed the impact of the extensive media coverage would
be significant and, for different reasons, did not trust the
journalists."

There was a sense that relitigating history would desta-
bilize it. But how *do* we stabilize the past? There's debate
over how exactly we should carry out what Irwin-Zarecka
calls "memory work"—the work of comprehending and
coming to terms with an event like the Holocaust. Is remembering enough, or is there a right, and a wrong, way
to remember?

I remember, and friends of mine remember, watching
a frightening short film in school called "The Wave," in
which a high school teacher shows his initially skeptical
students how the Holocaust could happen by inciting
them to participate in their own miniaturized version of
a totalitarian regime. (It's based on a real experiment that
took place in a California high school in the 1960s.) I also

remember visiting our local Holocaust museum with my humanities class in sixth grade; one particular detail the docent related, about the Nazis using Jewish prisoners' hair to stuff their pillows, made my best friend cry. (I might cry too, now, but I was more stoic back then.) If there was a didactic paradigm at work here, it intended to make the Holocaust real by making it personal.

The historian Michael Marrus has argued that viewing the Holocaust with a special sense of awe is counterproductive to historical understanding, because empathizing with the victims would "morally block" us from analyzing them critically. And attempts to situate the Holocaust in the context of other, seemingly comparable human atrocities, such as the Cambodian genocide in the 1970s, or the migrant detention centers set up in Texas in 2019, have drawn mixed response. On the one hand, it's dangerous to treat the Holocaust as a singular aberration in terms of the failure of cultural morality. (Because it has happened, it cannot happen again.) On the other, isn't it dangerous to treat genocide as a run-of-the-mill inevitability? (Because it has happened, it certainly will happen again.)

You're likely familiar with the concept of the phantom limb: After having an arm or a leg removed, a patient may continue to feel the presence of the limb, even feeling pain in it. Less familiar is the phenomenon of the alien limb, when a patient feels a loss of identification with their still-intact limb. When questioned, the patient might identify the arm in the bed as belonging to the nurse, for example, or they might claim that their leg is a "counterfeit" or a dummy leg.

The neurologist Oliver Sacks once sustained a leg injury while hiking and was left temporarily paralyzed in the leg. During this period, he experienced a kind of psychosis or hallucination, a persistent sensation that his leg was not his own or even real:

> I knew not my leg. It was utterly strange, not-mine, unfamiliar. I gazed upon it with absolute non-recognition . . . The more I gazed at that cylinder of chalk, the more alien and incomprehensible it appeared to me. I could no longer feel it was "mine," as part of me. It seemed to bear no relation whatever to me. It was absolutely not-me—and yet, impossibly, it was attached to me—and even more impossibly, "continuous" with me.

This sense of dissociation made recovery difficult, since, when he tried to walk, Sacks found he could not remember, or "think how," to flex the appropriate muscles. It was as though his leg had ceased to be a leg and in so doing erased its own history of legness: "The leg had vanished, taking its 'place' with it. Thus there seemed no possibility of recovering it . . . Could memory help, where looking forward could not? No! The leg had vanished, taking its 'past' away with it! I could no longer remember having a leg."

This bears some resemblance to the case of Jonathan I., a painter who suddenly lost his color vision at age sixty-five.

Sacks himself examined Jonathan I., and co-wrote, along with Robert Wasserman, a piece about him in 1987. Following an accident, the artist had become colorblind, but not in the usual sense of colorblindness, where one can't distinguish between reds and greens; he had lost *all* ability to distinguish color, such that the world to him appeared in grayscale, like a black-and-white movie. "My brown dog is dark grey," he said. "Tomato juice is black."

Having the color drained from his life deeply disturbed him. His own vivid paintings now looked muddy and gray to him, and had lost their meaning. Sex was unappealing—his wife's skin now looked "rat-colored"—and food was unappealing; he had to close his eyes to eat, but "this did not help very much, for the mental image of a tomato was as black as its appearance." That is to say, Mr. I.'s visual memory and visual imagery had lost their color as well; he knew which colors things were supposed to be, but he could no longer see those colors. He resorted to eating mostly black and white food, since white rice and black coffee at least looked relatively normal.

There's also the case of John M. Hull, who lost his sight at twenty-four and wrote a book about his experience, called *Touching the Rock*. After going blind, he began to lose his body image; unable to see his own body with his eyes, he became unable to imagine it: "The fact that one can't glance down and see the reassuring continuing of one's own consciousness in the outlines of one's own body," he writes, creates the sense that one is "dissolving," "no longer concentrated in a particular location."

Blindness also rewired Hull's visual memories; after some time he found he could no longer picture his loved ones, or even his own face. Other people became "disembodied voices," and his own being a disembodied self. Hull, too, lost interest in food and sex, basic drives that must be more visual than we realize.

Then there's the case of Monsieur A., who was studied by the French neurologist Jean-Martin Charcot in the late 1870s, and revisited by Israel Rosenfield in his book *The Strange, Familiar, and Forgotten: The Anatomy of Consciousness*. Monsieur A. had what is commonly known as photographic memory, more technically eidetic memory, an ability to recall visual memories in unusual detail. "If he read a book two or three times," Rosenfield writes, "he could visualize any page in it and 'read' it aloud from memory." Then one day he lost his visual memory— suddenly "everything appeared unfamiliar." His vision—his eyes—were perfectly intact. He could still *see*. But what he saw did not have visual meaning. His once highly accurate drawings done from memory became crude scribblings. His dreams became verbal rather than image-based. And there were more profound effects:

> He could not imagine his wife and children. At first he failed to recognize them, as he had the streets of his hometown, and then he said they seemed to have changed. Nor could he recognize himself in a mirror: walking in a public gallery, he suddenly noticed that his passage

was blocked, stepped aside, and excused himself. He was
looking at his own image in a mirror.

Monsieur A.'s disorder was an apparent breakdown
of the ability to construct new visual memories, but in
losing this, he also lost the ability to reconstruct old visual memories—just as Sacks forgot how to feel his leg,
Jonathan I. how to see color, and Hull how to see his own
face.

My husband, who is losing his hearing, tells me his auditory memories are losing their coherence. He says that
part of the reason one eventually gets used to hearing aids
is that you forget the way things sounded before—he can't
remember his favorite songs, he can't imagine how traffic or the ocean used to sound with natural hearing, un-
amplified and uncompressed. (Through hearing aids, he
says, the noise of traffic is nearly unbearable.) These stories
suggest that if through injury or illness we lose the code to
our memories, if we can no longer embody the method of
encoding, we lose the memories entirely. We forget how to
remember them. And then finally what was remembered
will lose its significance.

If this is true, "memory work" becomes even more cru-
cial. At the time she published *Frames of Remembrance*, in
1994, Irwin-Zarecka noted that "among the people actively involved in recent debates about the Holocaust, both
in Germany and Poland, most belonged to the generation
of war children, a generation with personal memories but

also no direct responsibility." This generation would feel keenly the necessity of remembering the Holocaust, without the undue burden of firsthand memory. "The elapse of time does make it easier to confront the morally challenging past," she writes, "yet it may also work to create a gap of relevance." A generation later, the gap has widened. Events that once seemed so indelible must seem remote now. We have not, perhaps, done the right work, passed on the right codes to decipher these memories. Or perhaps it's simply impossible to make historical memory feel sufficiently real that we won't have to repeat history.

I recently visited my parents for Christmas, and one night after dinner we were talking and drinking wine by the fire when my grandmother's house came up. I told my mother how I felt the house had never changed, was exactly the same as it must have been when she was a child. This was mostly true, she said, except for her bedroom. I had assumed this bedroom, which I often stayed in, contained the same furniture that was there in her youth. But apparently my grandmother reconceived it as a guest room in the early '70s. Some things were the same, like the green velvet loveseat that I always wanted. (I now own the loveseat, along with the melodeon and the floor lamp.) But in place of the double bed, with the elaborate canopied headboard, there had been two single beds arranged in an L shape in the corner; my mother drew a diagram on a yellow legal pad. "Which one did you sleep in?" I asked her. "That one," she said, matter-of-factly. "The other one was scary." (Why is it, when there's two of something in a house, one of them is always scary?)

Then my mother mentioned "the maid's room." My father and I were both confused—did she mean the laundry room, a small room off the den with an unfinished concrete floor, and a bare bulb with a pull-string, that also served as a pantry? (I remember six-packs of Tab on metal shelving.) No, she said, the maid's room—it was also off the den, but on the opposite side. We remained confused. She explained that when you walked into the den from the doorway to the kitchen, the maid's room was immediately on the right, behind swinging wooden doors. It was narrow, like a walk-in closet, but there was room for a cot.

I could not remember the room at all until my mother said it was where the placemats were stored. Then I had a flash of going in there as a child, pulling out the drawer that held the table linens, so I could set the table for some family dinner. I saw myself there in the little room, not from the first person, but as though watching a girl from a bird's-eye view or a hidden camera, out somewhere near the ceiling in the den. Yes, finally, I could picture the blond color of the wood and the way the drawer would often stick. But the memory was flimsy, like a memory of a dream. My father still could not picture the room; perhaps he had never been in there. "What do you imagine on that wall?" my mother asked. Just wall, we both said, a continuation of the wallpaper. I had no fond memories of that room, and in all my years of visiting the museum of my grandmother's house since it sold, had never seen it there; my mind simply wallpapered over it. And now I doubt the specificity of the rest of my museum—am I sure where the floor lamp was, of the color of the brocade?

Later, I recounted all this to my husband. "It's like that short story," he said, "'The Little Room.'" I had never read it, but I found it online. The story, written by Madeline Yale Wynne and published in *Harper's Magazine* in 1895, falls somewhere between supernatural horror and science fiction. A woman who is about to be married is telling her fiancé about "something queer that happened" in her childhood, and her mother's childhood. Her mother was raised in part by two half sisters who were nearly twenty years older than her, in Vermont. Later, she was sent to live with cousins in Brooklyn. Her fondest memory of the Vermont house was a "little room" that she remembered in great detail, having spent a couple of days in there once during an illness, being doted on: "the first time she had been of any importance to anybody, even herself." She told her own fiancé all about it, and when they went to visit her sisters in Vermont after their wedding, she couldn't wait to show her husband the little room. But in its place in the house, there is only a shallow china closet, holding gilt-edged china, and the sisters insist the house is exactly as it always was; there never was any little room.

They all have a good laugh about this, and assume the child must have imagined or dreamed the room: "When anything was lost they would always say it must be in the little room, and any exaggerated statement was called 'little-roomy.'" The really queer part, though, occurs years later, when the daughter, after her father has died in battle, goes to visit the house for the first time with her mother. The daughter, of course, is anxious to see the china closet. But when they get to the house, there is no china closet—there's a little room, exactly as her mother had remembered it as a child: the same wallpaper, the same blue chintz lounge with a peacock pattern. The mother, shocked, questions her sisters about the china closet, and they claim there was never any china closet there, always a little room; in fact, they don't even own any gilt-edged china.

Reading this story, of course I pictured the half little room, half china closet in my grandmother's den, just to the right of the doorway from the kitchen, where I can now see either wallpaper or a pair of swinging doors. It's like the optical illusion that is half rabbit, half duck; I can switch back and forth. You could say the story is about unreliable memory, the ultimate unknowability of the past, the impossibility of securing a single version of the truth. But it doesn't feel that way when you're reading it; it feels like the house in Vermont belongs to two realities. You don't know which reality you're in until you open the door.

2017

VANITY PROJECT

I have known for years that my "good side" is my left side—the arch of my left brow is a little higher, the left cheekbone a little sharper. That side began with an advantage and is gaining on the right all the time. In my teens, a mole appeared in the middle of my right cheek. It's not small enough, pigmented enough, or close enough to the mouth or eye to qualify as a "beauty mark," providing Barthesian punctum, the poignant accident; it merely mars my profile. I have a snaggletooth, my upper right lateral tooth, which began twisting out of line as soon as my braces were removed. It's cute, to a point. It sometimes catches on my lip when I smile. One morning just before my twenty-seventh birthday, I fainted and fell into a French door, breaking one of the panes with my face. The glass sliced my chin open, from lower lip to jaw, requiring fifteen stitches. The scar is on the right. My right side seems to be aging faster, inexplicably—the nasolabial fold is more pronounced—

though the left side gets more sun exposure in the car, and when I sleep on my side, I usually turn to the left.

It was only recently, however, that I realized I automatically look at my good side in the mirror. Because vision is stereoscopic—the two "beams" of your gaze converge at a point, rather than remaining parallel—you can't look someone in both eyes at once; you have to pick one eye at a time. Standing in a hotel bathroom, its mirror huge and immaculately clean, I noticed that when making "eye contact" with myself, I look at my left side. Reflexively, I gaze into my left eye.

There's a high probability that your face also has a good side, and that your good side is the left. Studies have shown that photographs of faces manipulated to be left-symmetrical (so both sides are the left side) are routinely judged to be more attractive than right-symmetrical faces, both in terms of reported "pleasantness ratings" and according to unconscious responses such as pupil dilation. One theory supposes that this is because the left side of the face shows more emotion: "Our results suggest that posers' left cheeks tend to exhibit a greater intensity of emotion, which observers find more aesthetically pleasing," researchers wrote. "Our findings provide support for . . . the notions of lateralized emotion and right hemispheric dominance with the right side of the brain controlling the left side of the face during emotional expression."

The photographer Julian Wolkenstein did a series titled *Symmetrical Portraits* in 2010, showing each subject's right-symmetrical and left-symmetrical photos side by side. The portraits are somewhat unsettling. The resulting faces look related but not identical, like sisters but not twins, and perfectly symmetrical faces dip into the uncanny valley, appearing alien, machine-like.

Comparing the half clones, I find the emotion theory plausible. One blond woman is, on one side, more conventionally attractive, which I suppose means more feminine—her eyes more catlike and farther apart, squinting slightly in a Tyra Banks–style "smize"; her nose narrower and pointier at the tip; her cupid's bow more defined. On the other side, she appears more androgynous, her overall countenance less taut. The androgynous side looks somehow less intelligent—but then, we routinely gauge more attractive people to be more intelligent (and nicer, and more competent), in the absence of other evidence; it's called the halo effect.

In a popular Quora thread, the top answers to the question "Why do I look good in the mirror but bad in photos?" all revolve around the "mere exposure effect": we tend to prefer familiar things simply because they are familiar. Photos often capture unfamiliar angles, but even taken head-on, like a mug shot, they show us our true face, not the reversed face we see in the mirror. It's the reflection that's inaccurate, but to us, the unreversed face looks wrong.

The best test we have for self-consciousness—which may be the same as consciousness—is something known as the mirror test. It's administered by putting a subject under anesthesia and then marking their face with an odorless paint. When the subject comes to, they are presented with a mirror. If the subject looks in the mirror and touches their face to investigate or remove the mark, we know they are self-conscious—they recognize the image in the mirror as themselves.

The mirror test has been performed on many different species. Chimpanzees pass the mirror test, but monkeys don't. Results with gorillas have been mixed. Dolphins and magpies also pass the mirror test. Children pass the mirror test, but not until the age of about eighteen months, at which point they also begin to demonstrate "self-emotionality," or self-conscious emotions, such as pride and shame.

I am fascinated by so-called mirror delusions, which can occur with brain damage or degenerative diseases like Alzheimer's. These patients cease, in a sense, to pass the mirror test; no longer recognizing themselves in their reflections, they believe their reflection is someone else— often an enemy. In *Stranger in the Mirror*, the psychologist Robert V. Levine describes a woman named Yolanda who became convinced that her reflection was a woman named Ruth. "I want her to come over but she doesn't want to come over," Yolanda said of Ruth. "I'm tired of talking to her through the window." She was described by her doctors as seeming "fond" of Ruth. Another woman, Donna, developed a much more antagonistic relationship with her reflection; she felt haunted by the "ugly hag" in the mirror, who would mock and mimic her. A third woman, R.D., felt similarly stalked by an "old bag" who "never told me her name": "When we get home, you know what? We're gonna find her waiting right around the windows. In the windows where she watches . . . I can't stand her."

Two of these women refer to the mirror as a window: If we don't see the reflection as ourselves, we may not notice that the glass is reflective. However, these patients typically persist in recognizing others in mirrors; they have not forgotten what mirrored surfaces do, nor do they have generalized prosopagnosia (the inability to recognize faces). It is only themselves they fail to recognize. Brain scans and autopsy reports reveal that patients like these almost always have right-side frontal lobe damage.

Another set of studies has shown that there is more right-brain activity when we encounter images of ourselves (what scientists call "the self-face") or hear our own voices. According to the psychologist Julian Paul Keenan in *The Face in the Mirror*, we also recognize our own faces faster when our right brains are active (which is tested by constraining the image to one visual field or asking the subject to respond with their left hand). This leads to the conclusion that the self, the sense of self, is not distributed throughout the brain but located in the right hemisphere.

I wonder, since the right brain controls the left side of the face, if we are drawn to left-symmetrical faces because they display not more emotion, but more selfhood? Do I look at my left side because I locate my self there?

Think of a memorable experience from your childhood. Do you embody your childhood self in the memory, or do you see it as though from across the room, or from a bird's-eye view?

There is something fundamentally different about mental images drawn from memory—when you picture a friend or a celebrity, say—and your self-image. The brain seems to build a self-model, a representation of your own body within your mind, so robust that you may glimpse or even confront your own "avatar" in certain fringe states of consciousness—dreams, memories, and fantasies where you watch yourself in the third person—and through the course of "glitches" in conscious experience, such as out-of-body experiences (OBEs) or autoscopy, the spooky phenomenon of seeing your own double.

What we see in general is not entirely the result of vision. The mind builds a model of our environment based on sensory input, which functions well for our purposes but is not identical with the "real world." Attention and assumptions play a large role in this, which is what causes "change blindness." In one well-known study, participants asked to focus on a task didn't notice when a man in a gorilla suit walked through the room. It's as though people are seeing a cached version of the world that, to save processing power, hasn't been refreshed.

According to the cognitive scientist and philosopher

Thomas Metzinger, our mind builds not only a world model but also a model of the self to exist in that world model— our inner avatar. In *The Ego Tunnel*, Metzinger posits that we need this avatar to experience selfhood. All experience is mediated, but we don't experience the mediation as such, in part because we identify so completely with this avatar. What we experience as direct access to the actual physical world through our actual physical body is really just an extremely immersive user interface. Rather than experiencing the world directly, we move through life in a kind of continual virtual reality.

This feeling of self-identification can be extended outside the body. In the famous rubber hand experiment, first devised by researchers at the University of Pittsburgh and Carnegie Mellon, participants were induced to identify with a rubber hand on the table when their own hand was out of view, behind a screen. In a paper published in 1998, Matthew Botvinick and Jonathan Cohen describe how each subject sat "with eyes fixed" on the rubber hand while the researchers "used two small paintbrushes to stroke the rubber hand and the subject's hidden hand, synchronising the timing of the brushing as closely as possible." The subjects reported that it seemed like they were feeling the sensation of the paintbrush in view on the hand in view— the rubber hand. These results have been repeated many times; the illusion is apparently so easy to re-create that you can do it as an impromptu party trick. People who use a cane every day or have artificial limbs experience a similar illusion. They don't have to think about where the cane is; they completely internalize the new dimensions of their "body."

This provides evidence for our mental ability to identify with an avatar—it's as though selfhood can float outside the body and latch on to something else. In a typical OBE, the "astral body," a doubled self, seems to exit the body through the head and hover near the ceiling so that it can view the now "empty" body below. Of course, you have not actually left your body; instead, the self-model seems to be replicating. These "replicants" may contain errors. Metzinger mentions an epileptic who, during a seizure, saw himself from the outside, wearing the same clothes but with "curiously" combed hair, whereas he knew his own to be uncombed.

Then there are phantom limbs. Amputees frequently continue to feel the presence of their missing limb and even feel pain in it, suggesting that the mental self-model can be so persistent and strongly ingrained that changes to the physical body are difficult to incorporate into a new mental model—that the mind is not as plastic as the body. Or perhaps it's that the sense of self expands more readily than it retracts, that the mind is resistant to reducing the scope of the self. I am reminded of the poet Anne Boyer remarking on Twitter that she did not identify with recent photos of herself because her hair was missing, following treatment for breast cancer. Of course, I thought: phantom hair.

How accurate, then, are our mental models? There's a pop-psych idea that people in general (women, especially)

are plagued by low-level body dysmorphia, believing ourselves less attractive than we really are. But there's evidence
to the contrary. One study found that people were more apt
to "recognize" themselves in photos when their images had
been enhanced—that is, photoshopped to appear more attractive. This points to an innate vanity. Maybe we prefer
our mirror image to photographs, especially candid photographs, because the reflection more closely aligns with our
self-model. The photograph is objective; the reflection is
enhanced. Further, change blindness could explain why

we appear old to ourselves on camera. We have grown old in real life but have been blind to those changes in the mirror; our mental model has not adjusted. When the delusional woman stops seeing her reflection as herself, her idealized self, she sees instead a mean old hag to be avoided.

My favorite variety of mirror delusion is known as "negative autoscopy." When this rare condition occurs, the patient—like a vampire—cannot see their own reflection in the mirror. To me, this has devastating implications, suggesting that what we see when we look in the mirror is not what is reflected at that moment but what we expect to see: our self-model. If we sustain damage to the area of the brain responsible for the self-model, we may be unable to construct a reflection.

And how much damage can the self withstand? The Cotard delusion, also known as "walking corpse syndrome," is a rare disorder in which patients stop using first-person pronouns and deny their own existence. This led one sufferer, known as "Mademoiselle X," to believe she was incapable of dying; she starved herself to death. Physiologically, it is thought to be related to the Capgras delusion, a form of prosopagnosia in which those with familiar faces are experienced as impostors. But here it is the self-face that is seen as an impostor. We no longer see or believe external confirmation that our mental self-model is real—a delusion that can lead to a catastrophic loss of self.

The proliferation of self-facing digital cameras makes it easier than ever to produce self-portraiture, to confront non-mirror-images of ourselves. When I tell my friend C that I'm writing about vanity, she tells me that she has taken a photograph of herself every day since she was twenty-seven, when she purchased a laptop with a built-in webcam. "I am obsessed with knowing how my face ages," she says, "and I want to know what my basic expression is." I have noticed that people who take and post selfies on the internet tend to choose photos from the same angle and showing the same expression. I think we must choose the photos that look most like our self-image; that self-image is then reinforced by the photos.

If I try, with my phone camera, to reproduce the image that I see in the mirror, I fail. The "live" camera shows me a mirror image, but once I take the photo, the image gets flipped, unreversed, my real face. My mirror image looks symmetrical to me, because I look at my left side and unconsciously assume symmetry. Only when looking at the photo do I see the asymmetry—the deeper crease on one side by the nose, the right eyelid drooping slightly. So I usually turn my face to the right, showing more of my left side. I keep my expression neutral, the neutral face I confront over bathroom sinks.

Some months ago, my friend A, then working on his dissertation, recorded me speaking about poetry on his expensive new DSLR camera and cut the footage into a short film. Some of the footage was shot outside a bar in daylight, that soft, late-afternoon light referred to dreamily by director-types as "the magic hour." This footage in particular horrified me. Supposed magical properties notwithstanding, the light seemed to magnify every flaw on my person: the facial scar, the sun damage, the second-day hair limp and stringy in the breeze, the tendency to frown and sneer while concentrating. It was not just that I found the angle or lighting unflattering, not quite to my standards—my reaction was vehement. I felt the person in this movie was hideously ugly, much uglier than my idea of myself, but more so, uglier than anyone I know. Though I knew it to be irrational, deathlessly vain, I was shaken to the core. I got drunk and cried.

Later, I read that people react strongly to images of themselves that they don't consciously recognize, often with powerful dislike. In one study cited by Keenan, men and women were shown images of their own faces and body parts (their hands, for example), without being informed that was what they would see, and were asked to rate their response. Some recognized themselves in the images and some didn't, but "non-recognition resulted in highly extreme ratings (for example, highly attractive and highly unattractive)," Keenan reported, noting that "subconscious recognition appears to have a strong influence." Perhaps my reaction to the video was a combination of recognition and non-recognition. I knew full well the woman speaking was me but could not square the visual with my mental self-image—the serene, impassive, almost expressionless face I find in a mirror or cultivate on camera.

My friend T once called me "beautiful by the conventional metrics," then added that he didn't mean it as faint praise—clearly intuiting that women, "intellectual" women at least, prefer to think of themselves as "unconventionally attractive." Until then, I had. But I am white and blond and thin. Had I flattered myself by thinking my looks interesting, even while identifying with my more conventionally attractive images? "'Conventionally beautiful' and 'not conventionally beautiful' both sound like insults," I said.

I like to be called beautiful in the moment, of course, but later I half resent it. I want, somehow, for others to think me beautiful without having to think of myself as beautiful—the myth of beauty without vanity. Being called beautiful has made me vain, not in the Narcissus sense, but in the sense of self-consciousness, much as being photographed makes me temporarily overaware of my body, my interface—"this mortal coil," I sometimes think of it. It is not what Shakespeare meant at all, but when I hear the phrase, I imagine my physical form is a skin I can shed like a snake.

I asked C to send me a few of her photos. She complied, writing:

> I'm sending you four pictures of myself—two new, two old. The difference is probably obvious. Here's what I see in them: I am simply more interested in life now than I was then. My lips used to be fuller and have gotten thinner. I think I used to look less like a specific person, more like a generalized girl, now I look like me more exactly.

"I used to look less like a specific person." "Now I look like me more exactly." I can see what she means. In the more recent shots, her gaze connects; it is piercing and intelligent. In the older photos, she seems to be trying to catch herself off-guard. I think of a woman I know who worked in door-to-door sales one summer; she was coached to be found looking off into the distance, as though distracted, when her mark opened the door. This was supposed to make her seem unassuming, less threatening. The goal was to get inside.

2016

WITCHES AND WHIPLASH

On Classical Hysteria

Before the twentieth century, it was common for women to suddenly lose the use of their lower limbs. They became unable to stand up and walk—this was called astasia-abasia—and as a result, they were forced to remain in bed. It was also common to experience the feeling of a ball rising up from the abdomen and into the throat. This was called globus hystericus, because it was thought to involve some kind of displacement or malfunction of the uterus. The sensation often led to "hysterick fits" or "vapours" or "fits of the mother" (the womb). "Fits" were usually characterized by "pseudoepileptic fainting and writhing about," as Edward Shorter puts it in his history of psychosomatic illness. "In fits," Shorter explains, "motor activity is apparently out of control, the limbs twitching histrionically, the eyes turned back in the head." But the term was also used to describe a "fashionable reigning distemper"—for example, throwing teacups into the fire.

The French physician Jean-Martin Charcot believed hysteria was a legitimate, inherited, and functional disease of the nervous system, an incurable condition whose symptoms included the aforementioned fits, or *la grande hysterie*. Patients in Charcot's clinic went through a familiar set of phases. First, they displayed the basic fits. Second, these would evolve into grander, more balletic movements—they'd leap around the room or contort themselves into "improbable positions," arching their backs to the point that only head and heels touched the ground. This stage was known as "clownism." Third, they would enter "a period of impassioned poses," such as prayer and crucifixion. The fourth, or terminal, phase was wild and unpredictable, and might include any of the previous symptoms as well as "demonic behavior." These women were oddly accepting of the hysteria diagnosis; doctors called their "unaffected composure" while describing their own symptoms *la belle indifference*, a beautiful flatness.

Hysteria is not a real disease. But patients learned these particular symptoms from accounts in the press as well as stories and novels about hysteria, which were popular in the late nineteenth century. This is not to say they were consciously performing the symptoms. However, when Charcot's theories were discredited—when the views of doctors such as Pierre Janet, who called hysteria a *maladie mentale* of the "highly suggestible," came into favor—the specific condition became much less common. Hysterical paralysis and "fits" were no longer part of the "symptom pool," in Shorter's terms—the symptoms made available to the unconscious by way of being taken seriously in the medical community. According to Shorter, patients didn't want to be seen as fakers or, worse, crazy. Once hysterical symptoms were believed to be "all in your head," women "stopped producing them."

The Freudian Conversion

"Hysteria" has hardly been scrubbed from the language, but "mental maladies" of the "highly suggestible" are now more properly termed "conversion disorder." The idea, taken from Freud, is that emotional stress or anxiety is unconsciously converted or sublimated into physical symptoms. These symptoms are often called psychogenic—originating in the mind—or psychosomatic—involving both the mind and the body (as all illnesses do; even a cold causes malaise, an uneasiness or mild depression). Conversion disorder is culture-bound, in that the physical symptoms of stress manifest in different ways in different cultures. Shorter notes that "patients' notions of disease tend to follow doctors' ideas—a kind of obedience." The relationship is "reciprocal"; patients and doctors inform and influence each other. But notably, patients want to please doctors, not the other way around; there's a power imbalance.

Some templates of sickness are available only to some cultures—take, for example, *koro*, a perception that one's sex organs are retracting, shrinking, or disappearing. It occurs most commonly in China and Southeast Asia but has also been seen in Africa, where it's often interpreted as "penis theft" and blamed on witchcraft. Premenstrual syndrome, on the other hand, seems to occur only in Western cultures. This changeability in the presentation of illness is sometimes called "pathoplasticity." But it's not just illness; most if not all behavior is culture-bound. The 1969 book *Drunken Comportment*, by Craig MacAndrew and Robert B. Edgerton, argues that while some results of alcohol, like clumsiness, are universal, "drunken changes-for-the-worse" differ greatly in different societies and eras. The sociologist Robin Room writes that whether or not alcohol is "banalized" in a society or saved for special occasions affects alcohol's "excuse value": "In Anglo-American and similar societies, drunkenness has some excuse value, but it is not a very good excuse." In other societies, intoxicated bad behavior "is likened to possession by spirits."

At one point, cultural ideas of disease spread primarily through word of mouth. Now the media plays a large role. Bulimia was unheard of before 1972, when a woman, a kind of patient zero, checked herself into a London clinic. The psychiatrist who treated her, Gerald Russell, "found her symptoms to be unique." In 1980, *bulimia nervosa* was included in the third edition of the *Diagnostic and Statistical Manual of Mental Disorders* (DSM-III). Several women's magazines published stories about the new bingeing and purging disorder, and then it spread like an epidemic. It was as though it had never before occurred to women that they could eat as much as they wanted if they simply threw it up.

Another example, Morgellons disease, is thought to have spread in part through the Internet. It was discovered, you could say, by a woman named Mary Leitao, whose two-year-old son had a rash inside his lips. Local pediatricians diagnosed it as eczema or atypical scabies, but it wasn't getting better. One day as she was rubbing her son's prescribed cream on the rash, Leitao noticed "something fiber-like" emerging from his skin, according to a story in the *Pittsburg Post-Gazette*. Leitao, a biologist, looked at the colored fibers "under an $8 RadioShack microscope" and was chilled. Leitao and her husband, an internist, decided their son had an unknown condition. They named it Morgellons after a description found in Sir Thomas Browne's *A Letter to a Friend*, published in 1690:

> Hairs which have most amused me have not been in the face or head, but on the Back, and not in Men but Children, as I long ago observed in that endemial Distemper of little Children in Languedock, called the Morgellons, wherein they critically break out with harsh Hairs on their Backs, which takes off the unquiet symptoms of the Disease, and delivers them from Coughs and Convulsions.

People who have, or believe they have, Morgellons complain of having itching and crawling sensations, as if of bugs, under their skin, and of finding fibrous materials like bits of string or foreign hairs in their sores. They often arrive at a doctor's office with a container of collected evidence—this is known as "the matchbox sign" or "the

Ziploc sign." The condition is often described as "controversial" and "unexplained." The official position of the CDC is that it's a form of delusional parasitosis, a fixed but unverifiable belief that something has invaded your body.

Conversion disorders are fraught not only because they are cultural—just describing a culture-bound syndrome can feel insensitive—but also because conversion is sometimes a last-ditch diagnosis when a "real" illness (conversion disorder is real) is not understood. When reading case histories of hysteria, it is very difficult to know if any given case was truly psychogenic. Some women who were believed at the time to have hysterical paralysis or fits quite probably had multiple sclerosis or epilepsy. And *globus hystericus*, or "the vapors"—which might involve belching, vomiting, back pain, lightheadedness, and fainting— sounds very much like a side effect of wearing corsets. As the etymology suggests, hysteria was overwhelmingly a woman's disease. Why was it always women and girls? One view is that women are more susceptible to conversion disorders because they're more suggestible than men. Another is that women have more emotional pain to convert.

The Realness of Pain

The neurologist Robert Scaer made a remarkable discovery while treating and studying patients with whiplash syndrome. These patients often seemed to be experiencing problems out of proportion to the severity of their accidents. One woman, Beth, had been in a car accident that occurred at only five or ten miles per hour; the cars were not damaged, and the other driver had no injuries. "Her insurance company was beginning to question her treatment," Scaer writes. But for months she had persistent and "terrible" neck and shoulder pain, numbness in one arm, and "disabling headaches." She ground her teeth at night. The pain began to radiate into her hips and legs. She had cognitive symptoms too, memory and concentration problems. She even developed a stutter.

Whiplash quickly earned a reputation as an insurance scam, an easy-to-fake condition that could be cured only by "the green poultice." But the whiplash pretender was a myth, like the so-called welfare queen. For the most part, Scaer's patients did not recover after receiving settlements. What made whiplash sufferers different from drivers who escaped these low-velocity accidents unscathed, Scaer found, was not greed but trauma. Beth, for example, when questioned about her early life experiences, told him that she had been raped by her older brother several times a week between the ages of six and twelve. She never told her parents because her father was an abusive alcoholic. "Similar to many of my patients," Scaer writes, "she was very open and candid and willing to share with me what must have been a hellish nightmare of her childhood." *La belle indifference.*

Another of Scaer's patients was in a low-speed but terrifying accident; while stopped at a light, with more cars behind her, she was forced to watch as a huge dump truck began backing up and crushed the front of her car. According to Scaer, a feeling of helplessness and a life threat are the two main criteria for trauma. (I thought of these prerequisites while watching Christine Blasey Ford's testimony before the Senate Judiciary Committee on September 27, 2018. She said, of Brett Kavanaugh, now confirmed to the Supreme Court: "I tried to yell for help. When I did, Brett put his hand over my mouth to stop me from yelling. This is what terrified me the most, and has had the most lasting impact on my life. It was hard for me to breathe, and I thought that Brett was accidentally going to kill me.") What Scaer had discovered was that whiplash is not really a physical injury but a form of PTSD. Whiplash is *emotional*. Almost all of Scaer's patients report losing "their sense of self" or having a "sense of unreality . . . often referred to as a 'fog.'" It's as if the accident provides an excuse to express the buried trauma.

People who have experienced trauma, such as sexual or physical abuse, are much more susceptible to retraumatization. It's not simply that they never get over the original trauma, although this is true. One study showed that circumcised boys are significantly more resistant to injections in the following months. Maybe they do "remember" the pain of circumcision. Trauma victims also, shockingly and unconsciously, engage in something known as "trauma reenactment." In one striking example of "anniversary syndrome," a Vietnam vet who inadvertently exposed his and his friend's location by lighting a cigarette, allowing his friend to be shot by a sniper, keeps attempting to rob a store, with a finger gun in his pocket, "on the exact day, hour, and minute" of his friend's death—"apparently unwittingly." Whiplash patients are apt to have more car accidents, maybe because they start overreacting, or underreacting—due to the "fog." One of Scaer's patients was in six rear-end collisions in the span of a year and a half.

This type of behavior might look from the outside like self-destruction or even self-fulfilling prophecy, a mysterious attraction to dangerous situations. From the inside, it seems to be a counterintuitive form of self-protection, like Stockholm syndrome. Abused children are prone to "inappropriate bonding" with their abusers—I think of the horrific memoir *The Incest Diary*, whose anonymous author admits that as an adult she still feels intense sexual attraction to her father, who began abusing and raping her when she was a toddler. During particularly painful episodes, she would float up and out of herself toward the sky—out-of-body experiences are common during trauma. Rats, Scaer notes, when given shocks in a certain part of a maze, will tend to return to that part of the maze, "leading to reenactment of the shock." He adds, "The familiar is more rewarding to the rats than the unknown." (I wonder if the author of *The Incest Diary* has read Scaer's work: "When an animal is scared," she writes, "it goes home, no matter how terrifying home is.")

The psychologist and trauma specialist Peter Levine developed a model of what you might call trauma avoidance in prey animals. He observed that when they're unable to flee or fight, they freeze instead—either hiding or playing dead. But while they are frozen, all the chemical activation associated with fight or flight persists. If the animal survives, once it's safe it will need to "discharge" this energy through shaking or trembling. He noted that humans also freeze in the face of threats, but rarely do they go through the discharge stage—likely because, as Scaer puts it, "dramatic shaking all over is 'unseemly' or 'hysterical,' and tends to be suppressed in advanced Western cultures." It's like the fight-or-flight process can't play itself out and so gets stuck.

Shorter would say that chronic pain is now part of the symptom pool, that the most likely ways for excess or unprocessed stress to be somatized in the twentieth century are as pain and fatigue. (Really, these symptoms were always available. A "hysteric" in 1760 complained in a letter of being "tired to death.") In *Hystories*, a smug, judgmental book I hated, the literary and cultural critic Elaine Showalter argues that chronic fatigue syndrome and fibromyalgia are modern-day hysterias we "catch" from the media. Scaer's work, though more clinical, feels deeply nuanced in comparison, and profoundly sympathetic in its reach for understanding. In his view, women report more chronic pain because they report (or do not report, but do experience) more abuse. (It feels very different to me, to call chronic pain a disease of stress, versus calling it hysteria—a matter of the locus of blame.)

To skeptics, psychogenic pain is somehow less real than other pain. But all pain is in the mind. In an essay on consciousness, the philosopher Galen Strawson introduces a thought experiment: "Suppose you're hypnotized to feel pain. Someone might say that you're not really in pain, that the pain is illusory, because you haven't really suffered any bodily damage. The reply is immediate. Truly to seem to feel pain just is to be in pain." Even chronic pain resulting from definite injury may be "illusory" in some sense. The neuroscientists V. S. Ramachandran and Diane Rogers-Ramachandran have described a "curious but tragic pain disorder" called complex regional pain syndrome. After an injury such as a broken finger, your hand is immobilized to allow it to heal. In a small percentage of cases, however, "the immobilization turns into permanent paralysis, and the hand becomes progressively more swollen, painful, inflamed and dysfunctional. The pain and paralysis spread upward to involve the entire arm. There is no known treatment."

Ramachandran and Rogers-Ramachandran believe that in these few "unlucky individuals," an "unconscious association" or "memory link" is formed between the triggering cause and the result, "so the brain just gives up: learned pain." Once established, this kind of pain is very difficult to unlearn. It's related to phantom pain, which occurs in 60 to 80 percent of amputees and might present as an excruciating "cramp" or other highly specific sensations in the amputated limb; one man whose right arm and leg had both been amputated said, "It's as if the skin of my arm has been ripped off; salt is being poured on it and then it's thrust into fire. I also sometimes feel as if the fingers on my amputated hand are moving uncontrollably, which is both extremely painful and embarrassing." Phantom pain is a fixed belief that the missing part is still there in some sense and also still hurts. And it does—if you believe you're in pain, you're in pain.

Placebo Effect

The symptoms of "hysteria" on record often read like conditions of somatic, not psychogenic, origin—like indigestion from wearing corsets, or endometriosis, or irritable bowel syndrome, or migraines. (Oliver Sacks's book on migraines suggests they can cause almost any symptom at all, from nausea to partial blindness to an acute and uncanny fear of death. Blaise Pascal would report the sense of a "precipice" "yawning" on his left-hand side—his friends called it *l'abime de Pascal*, Pascal's abyss.) But we now know, the thinking goes, that what the patients really had was conversion disorder, because they responded to bogus treatments. Shorter cites a woman in Bath in 1663 who suffered from debilitating weakness and joint pain. After "a vigorous round of enemas, laxatives, and bathing," she felt well for ten years—at which point she developed gout. Some of the more ludicrous treatments that "worked" to cure hysterics were the burning of feathers or asafetida (a pungent ingredient common in Indian food, it means "fetid resin") to somehow "treat the uterus," as though to smoke the monster out, and unnecessary, voluntary surgeries—there was a fad for a while of removing the ovaries, called Battey's operation. Women would supposedly beg or demand to be "Battey-ized."

There were also, however, involuntary surgeries, such as clitoridectomy, basically genital mutilation, performed as a cure for nymphomania, "which usually meant chronic masturbation," Shorter writes. In a "typical case from Paris" (he quotes from the case history): "A young woman was so given to masturbation that she was close to dying from exhaustion . . . In vain her hands were tied." They literally tied her up, but "she was able to gratify herself by rubbing against some protuberant part of the bed." (Perhaps this young woman had been abused? Children who are sexually abused often masturbate obsessively.) The case notes claim the patient and her parents both "readily agreed" to "amputation of the clitoris." The doctor "resected the organ with a single knife stroke" and then cauterized the wound with a hot iron. They pronounced her cured. (She probably did stop masturbating, or at least seeking medical help.)

In 1836, William Roots, a doctor on staff at St. Thomas Hospital in London, told a group of medical students: "You all know that nothing is more common, when a woman is hysterical, than to see her relieved for a time by the burning of feathers under her nose." But what Roots is describing is the placebo effect, which works for "real" illnesses too. When you are sick or in pain, being offered treatment—being taken seriously—itself offers a measure of relief. Responding to silly or arbitrary treatments would not preclude all "hysterics" from having somatic conditions. The placebo effect is especially strong when both doctor and patient believe the treatment to be effective. Some common drugs appear to work only when patients know they are taking them; a 2003 paper reported that diazepam, commonly known by the brand name Valium, has no effect on anxiety when administered secretly through a drip. But people who willingly take diazepam report significant reduction in anxiety.

It may seem straightforward, but the placebo effect is not well understood. In *13 Things That Don't Make Sense*, the science writer Michael Brooks describes a surprising experiment:

> It all kicks off with the pain-racked patients receiving something like a morphine drip. Later, after the patients have begun to associate the morphine with pain relief, you can subtly substitute saline solution for the morphine. The patients don't know their "morphine" is nothing but salt water and, thanks to the placebo effect, they report that their pain medication is still working fine. That is strange in itself, but not as strange as the next twist makes things. Without saying anything to the patients, you put another drug into the drip: naloxone, which blocks the action of morphine. Even though there is no morphine going into their patients' bodies, naloxone still stops the relief in its tracks; the patients, oblivious to all that has gone on, now report that they are in discomfort again.

This suggests that "the saline really was doing something." But what? Had it tricked the brain into producing its own morphine?

Also confusing matters, much of what we casually attribute to placebo could be regression toward the mean—statistically speaking, most people who feel unusually bad will eventually feel better. They'll regress back to baseline. So it may be that many hysterics would have gotten better

anyway, with or without the burning of feathers and re-
moval of ovaries. We can't really know whether, or how,
they were sick.

Demoniac Drama

If there is classical hysteria, there is also classical possession. In *The Devil Within*, the historian Brian P. Levack
outlines "the symptoms of early modern possession" in
Christian Europe, a pattern of symptoms that has notable
overlap with hysteria: convulsions or "fits"—"often accom-
panied by frothing or foaming at the mouth"; physical
pain, ranging from "minor irritations such as pinpricks
or the feeling that ants were crawling under the skin, to
those described as torments or torture"; "rigidity of the
limbs"; "muscular flexibility and contortions" (including
arching of the back—very Charcot); "preternatural strength";
levitation (as a symptom!); swelling; vomiting, especially "of
alien objects"—"pins and needles, nails, glass, blood, pottery,
feathers, coal, stones, coins, cinders, sand, dung, meat, cloth,
thread, and hair"; "temporary loss of sight, hearing, or
speech"; fasting; "demonstrations of linguistic facility,"
including speaking foreign languages—"Latin was sometimes referred to as the devil's tongue"; "belly speech,"
in which the possessed would emit an animal sound that
didn't seem to come from the mouth, or "barking like a
dog"; trances and visions; and clairvoyance.

During this period, people possessed by demons, or demoniacs, also tended toward blasphemy, cursing and beating or spitting on crucifixes. Any "immoral gestures and actions" were seen as a sign of possession. Possessed nuns would make "lewd sexual gestures" (one thinks of Linda Blair in *The Exorcist*, masturbating with a crucifix, yelling "Your mother sucks cocks in hell!") and in one case, "during mass in an Italian village demoniacs not only shrieked in animal voices and contorted their bodies but also pulled up their dresses" (the horror). Later on in history these symptoms or behaviors would most likely be seen as hysteria, but the "dominant contemporary interpretation" was that Satan "or one or more of his subordinate demons" had invaded the demoniac and taken control. The body, Levack writes, was viewed "as being porous or permeable and hence vulnerable to supernatural attack."

Demons were believed to be everywhere. "The earth swarmed with millions of demons of both sexes," Charles Mackay writes in *Extraordinary Popular Delusions and the Madness of Crowds*, first published in 1841. "The whole air was supposed to be full of them, and many unfortunate men and women drew them by thousands into their mouths and nostrils at every inspiration"—the medieval equivalent of the urban legend that you eat eight spiders a year in your sleep. Elias Canetti called these omnipresent spirits "invisible crowds"—because their numbers are always increasing, "a feeling of their density prevails." In *A Delusion of Satan*, a history of the Salem witch trials, the journalist Frances Hill writes, "Devils and spirits were not abstract ideas but creatures dwelling all around them. It was for this reason that Satan was sometimes referred to as the 'Prince of the air.'"

Some contemporary theories of the era of possession are that demoniacs were either sick (epileptic or schizophrenic, perhaps) or outright frauds. The latter interpretation makes sense, as you would think at least some of the "symptoms" of possession would need to be faked—the vomiting of broken glass or needles comes to mind (although I heard on the radio about a recent spate of "pranks" in Australia, in which people, apparently not just one "prankster" or psychopath but multiple copycats and even some children, were hiding needles in strawberries). But people with Morgellons disease, for example, are not frauds, collecting dog hairs for their matchboxes; they really believe there are fibers emerging from their bodies. And there might be: If you're constantly scratching all over, wouldn't it be easy to get bits of fiber from your clothing or bandages into your skin? And if you believe you're possessed—because your family and pastor and doctor think so—and you vomited on top of a needle or some trash, you might think, in the confusion, it had come from your body. These poor souls, according to Levack's theory, were "performers in religious dramas." Whether "unconsciously or not," they were "following scripts." They had *learned* how to be possessed.

Conversion Contagion

We now understand "hysteria" as conversion disorder, and mass hysteria—the madness of crowds—as contagious conversion disorder, or mass psychogenic illness. It's particularly common in small, tight-knit communities—in schools and in convents and in small towns, like Salem. And as with "hysteria," it's most prevalent among women or young girls. One highly publicized recent example occurred at a high school in Le Roy, New York, in 2011. It started when a cheerleader woke up from a nap and started spasming and twitching. It looked like Tourette's syndrome, but a few weeks later her best friend, another cheerleader, started showing the same symptoms. Soon more than a dozen students were sick, stuttering and flailing uncontrollably. One girl accidentally gave herself a black eye.

The students and their parents were terrified and angered by this sudden and debilitating condition. Why was it spreading? Was it a virus or the effects of some environmental toxin? It was variously blamed on poisoned cafeteria food, synthetic marijuana, contrails, and possession. Others thought the students (all but one were girls) were faking their symptoms. In a documentary called *The Town That Caught Tourette's*, one of the affected students says, "They assumed we were doing it for attention." Another scoffs, "Seriously, why would we fake this?" She has a point—on film they do look possessed or insane. Edward Shorter speaks of "the dignity that all disease confers," but tics do not look dignified.

Investigations of the school grounds did not uncover any toxins (Erin Brockovich got involved), nor could doctors find any biological explanation for the tics. Naturally, their doctors began to suspect contagious conversion disorder. There was a student at the school with "real" Tourette's, so the patients would have known what it looked like. The story was complicated, however, by a student at an entirely different high school, an athlete named Lori Brownell in Corinth, about 250 miles from Le Roy. Brownell's story is entangled with Le Roy's because of the similarity of her symptoms. A pretty, well-adjusted teenager, she suddenly developed convulsive, compulsive spasms; a clapping tic; and what she said felt like electrical shocks in her spine. Even when she was heavily sedated, the tics would continue. She also has a constant "nuh-nuh-nuh" vocal tic—when she speaks, it's as though she is always interrupting herself, often mid-word. Her mother admits, not without shame, to being annoyed by it—a confession and delivery I found touching. Brownell's symptoms got so bad she had to be pulled out of school and watched all the time. Her younger sister often fulfills this duty. "Because Lori can't be alone?" she says. Then quietly, after a pause: "It's insane."

A physician named Rosario Trifiletti heard about the Le Roy girls and became convinced they were experiencing pediatric autoimmune neuropsychiatric disorders associated with streptococcal infections (PANDAS), a post-infectious syndrome that, like late-stage Lyme, many doctors think "doesn't exist." (Presumably, any suffering that persists after treatment still feels like real suffering.) Trifiletti got in contact with the families in Le Roy and prescribed antibiotics. The clinicians in Buffalo who had been treating the girls (or not treating them, since they believed it was conversion disorder) found the PANDAS diagnosis very suspect. (One says, kind of scornfully, that patients always want "a magic pill" to make them better. Wouldn't you?) After taking antibiotics, many of the girls did begin to feel better—but of course you could argue that they were responding not to the drugs per se, but to being believed. Or that it was the placebo effect, or regression to the mean, or some combination. Either way, it suggests the proper "cure" for conversion disorder is not to tell the patients it's conversion disorder but to treat them for something else.

Lori Brownell, for her part, began a treatment for Lyme disease that included long-term intravenous antibiotics. Both she and her mother continued to insist she wasn't "crazy," that she wasn't making her symptoms up, which they must have been told by many doctors. What confuses me still is that no one seemed to think she had Tourette's syndrome. There's no specific test for Tourette's syndrome, no obvious way to rule it out, though it's typically not diagnosed until tics have been present for at least a year. According to the National Institutes of Health, symptoms of Tourette's syndrome tend to worsen in teens and then decrease in adulthood, but may change into other behavioral or mental disorders such as obsessive-compulsive disorder (OCD), generalized anxiety and depression, or panic attacks. The NIH also notes that Tourette's syndrome is more common in men, which makes me wonder if it's a form of conversion disorder we've simply decided to take more seriously.

In *Mass Hysteria in Schools*, the sociologist Robert Bartholomew traces the history of "bizarre behavior in schoolchildren" beginning in 1566, when about thirty young students, both boys and girls, at a Catholic orphanage school in Amsterdam began falling into "trance-like states" and acting like cats. They also experienced seizure-like spasms and threatened to drown themselves. Unsurprisingly, they were suspected to be the victims of possession or witchcraft.

Such outbreaks of contagious conversion disorder have occurred all over the world. In a small town in India in 2004, a group of girls "fainted for no apparent reason" and then started meowing and crawling on all fours. In 1971 in Malaysia, a group of girls who lived at a hostel near their secondary school were "stricken with mysterious fits." One of them, Eva, spoke "in a foreign voice and persona" during her fits—her speech grew "fluent and dramatic," and "observers noted that her words and demeanor were both mesmerizing and poetic." When a witch doctor was summoned, Eva began to negotiate; she said she would "accept nothing less than 'a human blood sacrifice' to appease the angry spirits." Conditions in the girls' hostel were less than ideal, Bartholomew points out. There was no electricity, and the school's headmaster was always conducting "surprise inspections," making inappropriate comments, and offering "unsolicited advice," such as "ordering them to toss their sanitary napkins over a nearby fence into an old mine shaft," which, they thought, would anger the spirit of the *jinn* who lived there.

Untenable living conditions and extreme academic stress are common themes in conversion disorder. Take, for example, the outbreaks of laughing that spread through multiple schools in central Africa during the 1960s. In 1962, three girls at a missionary school in a village near Lake Victoria were overcome by "an unusual feeling of giddiness" and began to laugh uncontrollably. The "laughing mania" spread to nearby schools over the following months. Sometimes the laughing turned to weeping, as though any emotional outburst would do. When the mania spread to Uganda, the symptoms changed. In addition to laughter and weeping, the students, many of them men, complained of "pain in the heart." Some of them repeatedly struck or even stabbed themselves in the chest to "alleviate the pain." They also got into fights, stopped eating for days, and "said they wanted to smoke cigarettes." "In short," Bartholomew writes, "they were breaking all of the school's taboos," then blaming it on orders from their ancestors, who would come to them in visions.

A psychologist from the University of Ghana finally determined that the students were acting out, albeit unconsciously, against the poor conditions at the schools—food shortages, dirty drinking water, overcrowded dorms, and little to no medical attention. In this light, mass hysterias represent what Canetti would call a "reversal crowd," a crowd that attempts to enact a revolution or mutiny. Mass psychogenic illness, like conversion disorder, doesn't strike randomly, but instead arises when people are unable to process their anxiety and stress. They feel powerless, so the unconscious drives them to attention-seeking, even frightening behavior—attention is a kind of power. The cheerleaders in Le Roy, it eventually came out, were all under unusual levels of emotional stress. They'd been reluctant to admit it, perhaps, and give more credence to the theory of conversion disorder. Or maybe they were just accustomed to acting like everything was fine. One girl's mother had undergone multiple brain surgeries. Another's father was an absent alcoholic. The girls weren't just flailing and ticcing either; they were in physical pain, not typically a symptom of Tourette's syndrome. One girl's mother said her daughter would cry because "the pain was so bad." Pain is a kind of emotion.

If pain can be contagious, so can despair. When Goethe published The Sorrows of Young Werther in 1774, a novel about an artist who falls in love with a woman who's already engaged, and subsequently shoots himself, it caused a rash of copycat suicides in Europe ("Werther Fever"). In 1935, Ruan Lingyu, a silent film star sometimes called "the Greta Garbo of China," took an overdose of sleeping pills, and three women committed suicide at her extremely well attended funeral. More recently, in the 2010s, there were multiple "echo clusters" of suicides at two high schools in Palo Alto. Many of the students who killed themselves did it after the fashion of the first: by jumping in front of a commuter train. The principal at Gunn High School told

Lee Daniel Kravetz, the author of *Strange Contagion*, "For many of the staff it's their ninth [suicide] in the last six years . . . We're going back into autopilot." I often see a numbness in the response to mass shootings—in the autopilot "thoughts and prayers" remarks of lawmakers who feign that nothing can be done, but also in my friends, in myself. There were over three hundred mass shootings in the United States in 2018. How do we stay shocked?

Gary Slutkin, an epidemiologist, believes that "violence is a contagious disease." He seems to mean this literally: "It meets the definitions of a disease and of being contagious—that is, violence is spread from one person to another" and "specifically fits the basic infectious disease framework." Certain culture-bound syndromes operate like hyperviolent forms of mass conversion disorder—"running amok," for example, a phenomenon seen in Southeast Asia and defined as "an episode of sudden mass assault." Someone, typically a man, will run around trying to murder everyone. *Grisi siknis* ("crazy sickness"), which is seen in indigenous Nicaragua, is similar. It "turns people into witches and they go crazy," according to one *curandera*, a traditional healer. People with *grisi siknis* might tear through a village destroying huts with their machetes, seemingly in a trance.

In *The Anatomy of Human Destructiveness*, the social psychologist and philosopher Erich Fromm calls these syndromes instances of "ecstatic destructiveness": "Suffering from the awareness of his powerlessness and separateness, man tries to overcome his existential burden by achieving a trancelike state of ecstasy ('to be beside oneself') and thus to regain unity within himself and with nature." Another example, Fromm writes, is "going berserk," which is "found among the Teutonic tribes (berserk means 'bear shirt')." He explains: "This was an initiation rite in which the male youth was induced into a state of identification with a bear. The initiated would attack people, trying to bite them, not speaking but simply making noises like a bear . . . It is rage for the sake of rage."

A relatively contained example of violent contagion occurred in Wisconsin in 2014, when two twelve-year-old girls attempted but failed to murder a third friend, despite stabbing her nineteen times, as a sacrificial offering to "Slender Man," a meme-like fictional character that originated on a "creepypasta" internet forum. ("Creepypastas" are "pieces of cursed prose and pictures that circulate online, waiting to contaminate and possess the next reader," according to an article about the *danse macabre* published in a journal of feminist studies.) "Although [Anissa] Weier had introduced [Morgan] Geyser to the Creepypasta website where they learned about Slender Man," one journalist wrote, "it was Geyser who later said they could become his proxies by killing a friend." Geyser could be schizophrenic—her father is. I watched a documentary about the case that included footage of Geyser's father softly sobbing while describing his vivid hallucinations. Weier, in contrast, seems otherwise sane, although she was sentenced to twenty-five years in a mental institution. She seems to have been pulled into a shared delusion.

What Is a Witch?

Witch hunts through the ages have been a dark combination of possession, hysteria, and mass hysteria narratives. "For a period of two centuries and a half," Charles Mackay writes, Europe lived under a mass delusion that witches were everywhere. He describes the goings-on at a typical witches' sabbath at some length; here are some highlights:

> At intervals, according to the pleasure of Satan, there was a general meeting of the demons and all the witches . . . The devil generally chose a place where four roads met as the scene of this assembly, or if that was not convenient, the neighborhood of a lake. Upon this spot nothing would afterwards grow, as the hot feet of the demons and witches burnt the principle of fecundity from the earth . . . In France and England the witches were supposed to ride uniformly upon broomsticks; but in Italy and Spain, the devil himself, in the shape of a goat, used to transport them on his back . . . No witch, when proceeding to the sabbath, could get out by a door or window, were she to try ever so much. Their general mode of ingress was by the keyhole, and of egress by the chimney . . . When all the wizards and witches had arrived at the place of rendezvous . . . Satan, having assumed his favorite shape of a large he-goat, with a face in front and another in his haunches, took his seat upon a throne; and all present, in succession, paid their respects to him, and kissed him in his face behind.

Witches, then, literally kissed the devil's ass. This movable feast, where "all manner of disgusting things were served up and greedily devoured," followed by unfettered dancing, would end "when the cock crew": "This is a summary of the belief which prevailed for many centuries nearly all over Europe." During these long years, tens of thousands of "witches" were murdered—burned, mostly, but some drowned or hanged.

"By their own confession, thousands of old women—and not only old women—had made secret pacts with the Devil, who had now emerged as a great spiritual potentate, the Prince of Darkness," the historian H. R. Trevor-Roper writes in an essay about the European "witch-craze." These confessions, of course, were often delivered under pressure of torture: "Torture was used to extract and expand confessions, and lenient judges were denounced as enemies of the people of God." To question the existence of witches in general or one witch in particular was not tolerated: "Perhaps these 'patrons of witches' were witches themselves." The courts that used torture got better confessions, with "more extravagant and obscene details." The methods of torture included the "witch-chair," a heated chair with spikes; denailing (that is, removing finger- or toenails) or driving needles under the nails; *tormentum insomniae*, or forced sleeplessness; a "ladder" or rack that stretched the body; and the *strappado* or *estrapade*, "a pulley which jerked the body violently in mid-air." Any "circumstantial evidence" that one was a witch, which might include "a tendency to look down when accused" or "signs of fear," was used to justify the use of torture "to produce a confession, which was proof, or the refusal to confess, which was even more cogent proof." Retracting your confession once the torture was stopped was also considered a crime. (Since any result offered proof, you'd think the torture was unnecessary.)

It must be said, though, that not all confessions of witchcraft were triggered by torture. Some confessors evidently believed what they said was true. Others may not have, but *wished* it were true. A real witch has power, the power to curse her enemies. In the early years of the witch-craze, these spells or curses were, in theory, what the courts were punishing. But later, it was not necessary for a witch to act on her powers—it became a crime of *being* rather than *doing*. To believe you were a witch, even if others didn't believe it, was punishable too: "The belief implied the will." The rule was death to all witches, "good" or "bad." One preacher, William Perkins, even claimed that a "good witch" was "a more horrible and detestable creature than the bad."

Why all this knotted, backward logic? A treatise titled *Malleus Maleficarum* (*The Hammer of Witches*), first published in 1487, declared in its epigraph that "to disbelieve in witchcraft is the greatest of heresies"—worse than being a witch? It would be as if *Mein Kampf* claimed that not hating Jews was worse than being a Jew—which might make a kind of twisted sense, since Hitler needed more Nazis than Jews. According to *The Encyclopedia of Witches and Witchcraft*, the book's sales were second only to the

Bible for almost two hundred years. (My husband once told me a story about going with a Wiccan friend to a party where the host was showing off a copy of *Malleus Maleficarum*. The Wiccan pointed at it with real disgust and said, "That's an evil book.")

In America, Salem has become the reference witch hunt, despite its scope being much smaller than Europe's mass slaughter. According to Karen Armstrong, who wrote the introduction to Hill's *A Delusion of Satan*, this is exactly why we latch on to it. The European witch-craze "is almost too large to grasp," she writes—like the Grand Canyon, which I found oddly underwhelming the first time I saw it as a child; it was just too big. "Precisely because the Salem disaster was on a much smaller scale, victims and perpetrators alike can become intimately known to us." Any kind of "mass hysteria" or "moral panic" is inevitably compared to the Salem witch trials—take the fears, accusations, and erroneous convictions of "Satanic ritual abuse" that swept through the United States in the early 1980s. I found a book about it called *Sex Abuse Hysteria: Salem Witch Trials Revisited*, with an illustration of angry Puritans on the cover, not to belabor the metaphor. (This book does have the decency to concede that most accusations of sexual abuse are justified.)

Trevor-Roper writes that "any society is liable, at times, to collective emotion." As in other cases of mass psychogenic disorder, the atmosphere in Salem in 1692 was one of fear and oppression. And as Armstrong notes, both were gendered: "The conviction that women had sex with demons and flew through the air to worship Satan in or-giastic parodies of the Mass showed a truly diabolic terror of sexuality and the female." Hill speaks to the psychology of the two little girls who started the witch hunt: "Among the children was an impressionable nine-year-old daughter, Elizabeth, called Betty, steeped in her father's Puritan theology that made terrifying absolutes of good and evil, sin and saintliness and heaven and hell. Unsurprisingly, she was full of anxiety."

Betty's slightly older cousin, Abigail Williams, "seemed on the surface a tougher personality, but in her own way she was just as fragile." The lives of these girls were "monotonous past bearing" and yet "for a young girl to exhibit anything other than docility would have been to stir fears she was thoroughly evil." They were forbidden to show displeasure, much less rage. To relieve their boredom, Hill says, they "dabbled in fortunetelling," including a method of divination that involved breaking an egg white into a glass of water: "It must have been terrifying indeed when the egg white went still and they realized, or one of them whispered, that it was shaped like a coffin." This frightening moment is what started the whole business— the children began having "hysterical fits," experiencing hysterical deafness or blindness, and barking or purring. Additionally, "any small accident" brought "huge pleasure and merriment." Like the African students with laughing sickness, the girls in Salem were breaking social taboos.

In *Crowds and Power*, Canetti speaks to the importance of "the discharge" in crowd dynamics: "the moment when all who belong to the crowd get rid of their differences and feel equal." Mass hysteria offers cathartic relief in the form of collective discharge, the way conversion disorder helps to discharge excess stress. (Scaer describes the case of a woman in a car accident who developed gastrointestinal symptoms with no clear primary cause; they went away after trauma therapy but were replaced by anxiety attacks, nightmares, and a phobia of driving—in other words, conversion disorder *works*. It "takes off the unquiet symptoms of the Disease.") After succumbing, consciously or not, to all this very bad behavior, the Salem girls were likely more scared than ever, scared of death and of hell and of worldly punishment. So they blamed their possession on witches. While the witches stood trial, making their denials, the girls would writhe about the courtroom, apparently convinced each "defendant" was summoning demons to cause them injury. They cried and screamed that they were being bitten or pinched, their bodies forced into painful contortions. (Pain is an emotion.)

In the end almost no one was safe, but the first to be accused were ironically among the most powerless people in the village, including Sarah Good, a beggar; Sarah Osborne, who was "bedridden and possibly senile"; and Tituba, Samuel Parris's Caribbean slave. In Salem as in Europe during the witch-craze, ugliness, old age, and poverty were all seen as evidence of witchery. (Again, the logic seems backward: Wouldn't a witch use her powers to better her lot?) Because "the old ethos of helpfulness toward neighbors was in conflict with the growing emphasis on fulfilling individual needs and desires," Hill notes, supplicants or anyone who needed assistance created feelings of guilt, which then turned to anger and resentment. This view did not go away after the witch hunts. From the mid-1700s through the 1970s, a set of ordinances known as "ugly laws" essentially outlawed poverty as well as disability. In 1881, for example, Chicago made it illegal for "any person, who is diseased, maimed, mutilated or deformed in any way, so as to be an unsightly or disgusting object, to expose himself to public view."

When the Salem witch trials were over, twenty accused witches had been executed, most by public hanging. As Sarah Good climbed the ladder to her death, a man named Nicholas Noyes heckled and badgered her to confess. She told him, "I am no more a witch than you are a wizard, and if you take away my life, God will give you blood to drink." Noyes reportedly "died some years later of internal hemorrhage, bleeding from the mouth." (Finally, some witchcraft that worked.) The witches had hoods placed over their heads, "not to prevent their seeing the crowd but to prevent the crowd's seeing them." Death by hanging causes "swelling of the face," Hill writes, and "a bloody froth or frothy mucus escaping from the lips"— reminiscent of the "symptoms" of possession. Their bodies were then "disposed of in the crevices in the rocks at the side of the hill" in lieu of proper burying. Others went insane or died in "the witch jail": "As the most dangerous inmates, the witches were kept in the dungeons," which were likely infested with rats. The wardens treated them like animals, like "fair game for sadism," since they were "enemies of God." Dorcas Good, Sarah's daughter, was only four when she got this treatment, chained to a wall. At best, those released were financially ruined, since inmates essentially had to pay for their own room and board while incarcerated.

You might say the mania officially ended with an incident on Ipswich Bridge. The accusers who had testified in the witch trials passed an old woman and—maybe by habit—"went into fits." But the bystanders to this implied accusation "merely stared or hurried past." So the girls had no choice but to move along. "They had at last lost credibility," Hill writes. It is almost sad. They had also lost their very temporary power. It had been less than one year.

Coda: The Unreality of Emotion

As I write this, I'm home alone in early October. John is back in New England, for a spell, where it's warm if not hot. Here in Denver there's been a freak early snow, except not very freak, because it's snowed once in October almost every year since we moved here, seven or eight years ago, a snow that hits when many of the trees are still leafy and green; the boughs get too heavy with the weight of the snow and break off and scatter over the road. It's cozy inside, and all weekend I burn candles and write for eight or nine hours a day. My witch books are due back at the library early—someone keeps requesting them. From time

to time while I'm writing, often in the middle of compos-
ing a sentence, I'll spontaneously get up from my chair and
start pacing around the apartment. I don't know that I'm
going to do it before I do it. I don't have free will.

I've been crying more than usual lately. My insomnia is
worse than ever. If I'm still awake after 5:00 a.m., when it's
officially morning, officially tomorrow and "past bearing,"
I'll often start crying. It's not a crying from sadness, but
the crying helps; there's a painkilling effect. One night,
playing around on my phone in bed, I discover a YouTube
video of a young girl singing a cover of a pop song on a
Ukrainian reality show. She sings with an accent, but the
verses are in English: *Strangers are coming*, it starts. *They
come to your house.* The performance is mesmerizing,
climaxing with a transition from throat singing to a kind
of primal scream or falsetto shriek with reverb. Her vocal
coach starts to break down when she sings *Don't swallow
my soul* in the pre-chorus. Later she leaps from her chair,
ecstatic. Catharsis! I watch it ten or twelve times before I
fall asleep. The next day, I send it to a friend, who writes
back to tell me the song, "1944," is about forced migration
and ethnic cleansing under Stalin.

I took too many notes for this essay, almost fifty pages
of them. I'm not trying to brag but admitting an error. I'm
tired of reading through them; I keep finding lost threads.
I wanted to talk about familiars, and Lilliputian hallucinations, and voodoo death—also known as psychosomatic
death. Cliques and popularity, the invention of the vibrator,
"the paranoid style in American politics." I wanted to talk

about *Ghostwatch*, a mockumentary about a haunted house (in the style of the 1938 radio broadcast of Orson Welles's *War of the Worlds*), which aired on BBC1 on Halloween of 1992; it was banned for ten years, according to the BBC, because it gave some children PTSD and led to at least one suicide. I wanted to talk about Lisztomania and Stendhal syndrome, but they feel too light—although Lisztomania at the time was considered a real contagion. In his book *The Virtuoso Liszt*, the musicologist Dana Gooley warns against comparing it too closely to "Beatlemania": "When the word 'Lisztomania' was coined, the medical valences of the term 'mania' were still strong, whereas in modern parlance it designates any popular fashion or craze, and scarcely bears a trace of medical discourse." I'm not so sure; during the height of Beatlemania, women would often faint and collapse.

When I turned on the livestream of Brett Kavanaugh's confirmation hearing, I expected to feel angry. Instead, I cried through the whole thing. Like Christine Blasey Ford, I was assaulted at a party in high school, but I don't think that's the reason. It was just hard to watch—so evidently difficult for Ford to give her testimony, but she felt she had to do it, even though it likely would not prevent Kavanaugh from being confirmed. (It did not.) At one point, during a break in the hearing, CSPAN let through a caller who practically spat out, "She's obviously *lying*," and my tears turned to sobs at the sound of the word, the viciousness. *Believe women* runs like a refrain through my head, while I'm reading about hysteria and whiplash and witch scares, and even "Satanic ritual abuse" (one book includes a subhead, in all caps: CHILDREN ARE LIARS). The prosecutor brought in to question Ford implied that her polygraph test was compromised because her own lawyers paid for it. This was witch-hunt logic: If you fail the test, you're a liar; if you pass the test, it was faked. The prosecutor might have argued, but didn't, that polygraphs are inherently unsound, like torture.

Throughout the movement, #MeToo has been painted by some men and even some women as a witch hunt or a moral panic. In *Crowds and Panic*, Canetti classes crowds into types according to their "prevailing emotion," such as "flight," "prohibition," or "feast." It's an interesting conception of emotion. One of these types is the "baiting crowd": "The baiting crowd forms with reference to a quickly attainable goal . . . This crowd is out for killing and it knows what it wants to kill." Opponents treat #MeToo as a baiting crowd, the so-called social media mob. The movement has elements of the flight crowd ("created by a threat") and reversal crowd (demanding justice or revolution). But it may, too, have elements of the baiting crowd. When people are repeatedly wronged and have no formal recourse to stop it, they resort to grassroots justice, which overcompensates because it has to, to make an example of someone—if ninety-nine people don't get caught or don't get punished for their crimes, the hundredth person, we somehow feel, should pay one hundred times the price. Canetti speaks of baiting crowds that actually kill their victims, as in real witch hunts: The "permitted murder

stands for all the murders people have to deny themselves."
Writing in 1960, he said that "disgust at collective killing
is of a very recent date." We've substituted collective humiliation, public ostracization. The crowd offers absolution,
through diffused responsibility. "It is so easy and everything
happens so quickly."

Months ago, maybe years, I read an interview in *The
Atlantic* with Frank Bures, the author of *The Geography
of Madness*. The interviewer and the author were talking about whether certain culture-bound syndromes were
real—not a straightforward question. Then the interviewer,
Julie Beck, said something I've never forgotten: "There's a
debate among psychologists about whether emotions are
real, biologically innate things, or whether emotion is a
concept that humans made up, like money." I felt shocked
by that, and still feel shocked. Don't even infants have
emotions? If our emotions are a construct, what part of our
conscious experience is not?

Once, accused of coldness in my poetry, I wrote,
"Maybe emotions *are* ideas"—a defense of the cerebral,
an attempt to reduce all expression to thinking. Now
I'm closer to believing the opposite is true, that ideas are
emotions—that thinking is reducible to feeling.

2018

SLEEP NO MORE

In my midtwenties, I contracted HPV, like most sexually active people do at some point in their lives. Some never know they have it; for most, it goes away in a year or so on its own. My case was stubbornly persistent. Several years ago, after almost a decade of abnormal pap smears and cervical biopsies—tests that, although preventive and although I have insurance, cost me thousands of dollars over the years—a gynecologist finally told me that the dysplasia had progressed to the point that it looked precancerous. The time for cautious vigilance had passed. She recommended a loop electrosurgical excision procedure (LEEP) to remove all the abnormal cells, which usually serves as a cure. The procedure would be quick and could be done in her office under local anesthesia, like getting a filling.

My first colposcopy—a next-level pap smear, in which the doctor examines your cervix with a magnifying scope—was shocking. The doctor—who was very sweet and called me *Honey,* and whom I never saw again—used a comically huge scissors-like implement to snip pieces of my cervix off wherever it looked weird or inflamed, so they could be tested for cancer. There was no anesthesia; I hadn't even brought ibuprofen. I've heard doctors say there aren't many nerve cells on the cervix, and it's true that the snips don't continue to hurt in the same way a bad cut on your hand keeps hurting; you can't quite tell where the injuries are located. But there was nothing my body liked about the biopsies; each snip registered as cause for great alarm. It makes me think of those studies showing that plants give off distress chemicals and behave defensively (shrinking back, say, or producing substances that make them taste bitter) when you cut them; even a cabbage knows you're hurting it.

I assumed, given the anesthetic, that the LEEP would be no more painful than the biopsies I'd become more or less inured to over the years. Beforehand, I may have taken a Valium, as a kind of good luck charm; it doesn't work wonders on me. Things went worse than expected. The bizarre chair they had me in—not the paper-lined flat table with stirrups that is standard for vaginal exams, but a kind of modified dental chair with adjustable leg rests—looked like it was from the 1950s. My legs were propped up and spread apart, but the hinges, or whatever, on the left leg part weren't locking and it kept suddenly falling down, so my knee would drop a few inches. The initial shot of anesthetic from a giant needle hurt quite a lot; I'm sure my tension didn't help. In any case, the anesthesia didn't really take, or they didn't use enough. When the doctor touched the little electrical wire to my cervix, tears immediately streaked down my face; it felt like she was tattooing my reproductive organs. The room smelled like burning. A few minutes in, when the nurse asked how I was doing, I saw no reason to lie. "I'm kind of suffering," I said. This brought about no change in the procedure. It probably lasted ten minutes. Afterward, I got dressed, went down to my car, and let myself cry with abandon.

Sadly, that was not the end of that. My follow-up tests showed they hadn't gotten all the bad cells off and out, and I would have to do the LEEP thing again. It was the nurse practitioner, not the doctor who had wielded the electrosurgical instrument, who relayed this to me. She was a sympathetic woman and evidently felt bad about what I'd gone through. She said that, if I preferred, we could do the second procedure in the hospital under what's called "conscious sedation"—not the same as full anesthesia, but I would be more comfortable. I'm not sure why I wasn't given this option in the first place, but obviously I took them up on it.

When I got home from the follow-up appointment, I googled "conscious sedation." What I wanted to know was, how conscious are you exactly? The usual medical sites, WebMD and the like, weren't very clear on that question. I called my dad, an internist, and asked him what he knew about it. He seemed to think you were, basically, conscious, but that the drugs they gave you had an effect like laughing gas—you're enjoying yourself so much you don't really care, and later, as if you'd been drunk, your memory is hazy. My mom was present when my dad had a small patch of stage 1 melanoma removed from the center of his back under conscious sedation, and she said he was laughing and joking like he'd had "a few margaritas."

The second procedure was definitely more involved. I had to get a physical and an EKG to clear me for surgery; nothing by mouth after 10:00 p.m. the night before. I arrived at the hospital before 6:00 a.m. In the pre-op room, I met the gynecologist who would be doing the surgery—she was part of the same practice, but not the one who'd performed the procedure in office (who maybe, I theorized vaguely, didn't want to deal with me again). This doctor had smooth dark hair; her manner was firm, efficient, and elegant. I also met the anesthesiologist, who was tall and thin and graying and seemed—I don't know how else to put it—like a fun guy. He asked me if I'd ever had conscious sedation before. When I shook my head no, he said, "Okay, you'll sleep through this." He was very clear on that: I'd wake up, or they'd wake me up, in the recovery room. He told me his "poor wife" had also had a LEEP under local anesthesia and hated it. We spoke for a few minutes and he left.

I saw him again just after I'd been wheeled into the bright-white operating room; the elegant gynecologist was near my feet, and he was standing over my head, with a surgical mask on. "I just slipped a little something in your IV," he said. That's the last thing I remember, until I was back in the recovery room, where they waited until my blood pressure was high enough that I could stand and walk around without fainting before they let me pee. Before I left the hospital to go home and sleep off the rest of the sedatives, the gynecologist dropped in to tell me everything had gone very well, but I saw no more of the anesthesiologist.

The next day, I felt like I missed him.

When I was fourteen or fifteen, my mother told me her mother had had both her children under the influence of "twilight sleep," the dreamy English translation of *Dämmerschlaf,* as it was called by its inventor Karl Gauss. What my grandmother said was that she'd gone to sleep and when she woke up she had a baby in her arms. The "sleep" was induced by a combination of scopolamine and morphine. However, while it may have felt like sleep to the patient, it didn't necessarily look like that to others. My mother, who has a PhD in history, sent me some documents on twilight sleep from her files, including this snippet from the book *A Woman in Residence,* by the physician Michelle Harrison, who graduated from medical school in 1967:

> When I was in medical school, the ward patients in labor received little or no pain relief, while the private patients were given scopolamine, a drug that wiped out the memory of the labor and birth. Many women loved it and would say, "My doctor was wonderful. He gave me a shot to put me out as soon as I came to the hospital. I never felt a thing." Those women weren't put out, but they didn't remember what had happened to them—at least not consciously. When these women thought they

were "out" they were awake and screaming. Made crazy from the drug, they fought; they growled like animals. They had to be restrained, tied by hands and feet to the corners of the bed (with straps padded with lamb's wool so there would be no injury, no telltale marks), or they would run screaming down the halls. Screaming obscenities, they bit, they wept, behaving in ways that would have produced shame and humiliation had they been aware. Doctors and nurses, looking at such behavior induced by the drug they had administered, felt justified in treating the women as crazy wild animals to be tied, ordered, slapped, yelled at, gagged.

She also sent me a scholarly article called "Birthing and Anesthesia: The Debate over Twilight Sleep" by Judith Walzer Leavitt, which includes a photograph of a woman from 1915 in a white garment, captioned "Gown with continuous sleeve"—her arms are safely trapped inside a single unbroken loop of fabric in front of her, like the party favor that used to be called "Chinese handcuffs." This presumably would limit her thrashing.

When my mother talks about twilight sleep in her class on gender, health, and medicine, her students tend to react as though this once common practice was obviously inhumane, possibly dangerous, and perhaps misogynistic too. But it's not clear, from what I've read, that these women or their babies were under special risk; scopolamine and morphine, after all, are still in use, in other medical contexts. In *The Worst of Evils: The Fight Against Pain*, Thomas

Dormandy, a professor of pathology, notes that "even by the most cautious standards" the doses of morphine used in twilight sleep "posed no threat to any infant." And Leavitt argues that women in the early twentieth century viewed twilight sleep as a liberating choice; they were finally being given the option not to suffer. In a 1999 review of a book about medical and social responses to childbirth in *The New York Times*, Ann Finkbeiner writes that the practice was "killed off by antichemical sentiment" in the 1960s. Awareness—control—during childbirth came to be seen as a feminist issue. My own mother had both me and my brother in the late 1970s through so-called natural childbirth, with no anesthetic.

It's also not entirely clear how different twilight sleep is from other forms of anesthesia. Take conscious sedation—I looked it up again recently. This time, I found a Medscape article that claimed the terms "moderate sedation" and "procedural sedation" were now preferred. According to this article, procedural sedation involves drug-induced "depression of consciousness" but only to a degree: "Patient responds purposefully to verbal commands"; "Spontaneous ventilation is adequate"; "Cardiovascular function is usually unaffected." A handful of different drugs can be used in combination to achieve these effects. They include midazolam (a benzodiazepine that can make people "chatty"; this is probably what my father had), fentanyl or morphine (opioids), and sedatives such as propofol. In pediatric surgery, ketamine is sometimes used, as it doesn't typically cause delirium or dissociative states in children. These drugs relax the patient; relieve pain; and, importantly, erase or at least obscure any memory of the procedure.

The amnesia can begin while you're still quite conscious. In *Anesthesia: The Gift of Oblivion and the Mystery of Consciousness*, Kate Cole-Adams quotes an anesthesiologist who reports that "conscious sedation can very well include conversation . . . even if the patient has no memory of it. Most often I spend the time at the end of conscious sedation cases answering the same questions over and over . . . They are sedated but have no recall." As Cole-Adams puts it, they "can hold onto old memories" but "lose track of new memories within seconds." So it's like being blackout drunk: Your body and mind go on doing things, making (potentially bad) decisions, but later you feel as if you weren't even there, not just that whatever happened to you didn't happen to you, but that what you did yourself didn't happen to you. (A friend of mine tells me that Koreans refer to blackouts as "the film being cut.") Like many—maybe all—aspects of anesthesia, the nature of this induced amnesia isn't fully understood. In his book *Counting Backwards: A Doctor's Notes on Anesthesia*, Henry Jay Przybylo writes that "debate exists as to whether the anesthesia experience prevents memory formation or memory retrieval." So it's possible that the memories form but go somewhere inaccessible, or less readily accessible. He calls the gap a "time hole."

I once mentioned on Twitter that I had warm feelings about anesthesiologists, although I've only knowingly met the one. A number of women responded that they had very different sentiments. One wrote, "When my anesthesiologist learned my husband worked at a design/build firm he—while prepping me—pulled out a copy of *Architectural Digest* to ask my husband's opinion on a lamp. (Husband told him to focus on keeping me alive and choose decor later.)" Another: "Mine almost refused to give me an epidural after I flipped him off—mid-contraction—when he asked if I really wanted one." A few agreed, though, saying their anesthesiologist had been "really hot" or "super hot." In the course of her research, Cole-Adams (a journalist and novelist, not a physician or scholar of medicine) meets one named Chris Thompson, whom she comes to think of as "Mr. Anesthesia"—his eyes are so "startlingly intense" that she goes into "a kind of trance" as she speaks to him and finds it difficult to concentrate. It sounds like the pseudo love-spell that mine put on me. I had come prepared with questions but didn't ask very many. I wanted to trust him, and I wanted him to like me. It was maybe my briefest-ever crush.

Moderate sedation, like twilight sleep, can be disinhibiting: "It is not unusual for patients, just before passing out, to tell surgical staff how attractive they are, to invite them on dates or even to bed," Cole-Adams writes. Some women awake from propofol reporting elaborate sex "dreams" and even orgasms. (Whatever anesthetic unconsciousness is, it isn't sleep.) Others, troublingly, may believe they have been assaulted during surgery. This would be unlikely now, since surgical patients are legally prevented from being alone with a doctor during a procedure—doctors want this legal protection as much as patients—but in the early days of anesthesia, perhaps until recently, this certainly occurred. There are also contemporary cases of medical professionals using propofol, sometimes on their girlfriends or wives, as a "date-rape drug." (I hate the term "date rape." If you murder someone on a date, it's not called "date murder.") In the 1800s, according to Dormandy, "it was widely felt that 'anesthetic intoxication' posed a special threat to women." Anesthesia was "of the devil." It was not just that women "were liable to be raped," but that "under the influence of the drug genteel ladies might attempt to seduce their anesthetist." And while "drunk on ether or chloroform, respectable women sometimes did the most shocking things" or "might experience distressing fantasies." Distressing to whom, one wonders? It makes me think of the young women, sometimes nuns, in medieval Europe whose lewd gestures or sexual remarks were considered signs of demonic possession. It's not that evil was liberating so much as that women's liberation looked evil.

Most anesthesiologists insist that general anesthesia, the full "going under," is not just apparent unconsciousness (since the mix includes agents that induce physical paralysis, so the patient doesn't twitch while under the knife) plus amnesia. They insist that the depth of unconsciousness precludes "feeling" anything. But there are many reported cases of what sounds like temporary locked-in syndrome in the operating room. These patients report being "awake" during the whole procedure, in screaming pain and yet unable to scream or move or even blink to alert the medical staff of what's happening. Cole-Adams relates a story she heard from a woman named Rachel at a dinner party, the story that triggered the author's obsession with anesthesia. Rachel had undergone a caesarean section during which the anesthesia appeared to have failed; she endured it "conscious, paralyzed and in agony." Rachel "realized she was not breathing" but not that a machine was doing the breathing for her—she had the sense that if she couldn't get a breath, she was going to die. But she also felt sure the pain itself was going to kill her. She had to force herself into a kind of out-of-body experience to cope with the pain, but instead of leaving her body, the source of the pain, she went further into it: "There was a feeling of going down, a feeling of descending . . . deeper and deeper into the pain." This didn't lessen the pain, she said, but she "no longer really cared about it." (The protagonist of Kristen Iskandrian's novel *Motherest*, after receiving an epidural, thinks, "The pain became more storied—I knew it was happening but it wasn't happening to me.") Eerily, when Rachel saw her baby, she said, "You know that newborns have such a black stillness in their eyes . . . I felt like she'd just come from where I'd been." (I wrote in the margin, *Hell?*) In another, "famously horrible" case in Cole-Adams's book, a musician named Carol Weihrer reports being awake during eye surgery, feeling her eye being "scooped and wrenched from its socket" and "the optic nerve being severed"—an experience so profoundly traumatic that she no longer lies down.

There have been many experiments to try to determine

how conscious patients are, or can be, under general anesthesia—for example, the surgeon might say something quirky, then later creatively test to see if the patient has any memory of the remark. (Sometimes these experiments are unintentional—Cole-Adams cites an incident in which a surgeon complained during a procedure about "black stuff"—mold—in his shower; the patient became convinced that the surgery hadn't gone well because they didn't get out all the "black stuff.") These studies have conflicting results and are often not reproducible. (But then, most scientific experiments have proved unreproducible—what's known as the "replication crisis." Much of what we call science is questionable.) If they are a little conscious, could they experience pain in the moment, and just not remember it, or remember it well, afterward? Anesthesia requires a delicate window: too little and the patient might be traumatized—the powerlessness often leading to a persistent, uncanny loss of sense of self—too much and they might not wake back up. That's why you can't just add more ether to cover your bases. But some doctors think that even pain you don't consciously "feel" can be remembered. The anesthesiologist Daniel Carr believes that "the memory of pain—the body's memory of pain, that is—can be more damaging than the original experience." He cites experiments showing that shocking a giant sea slug in the same place you shocked it previously causes a more complicated pain response—implying more pain—than the original shock. The pain researcher Clifford Woolf similarly thinks that "even unconscious pain" can "trigger chronic responses in the spinal cord that . . . later coalesce into pain"—conscious pain, that is—lasting months or years after the operation.

"Unconscious pain" is an interesting construction, almost a paradox. Galen Strawson has written, "To seem to feel pain just is to be in pain." But the converse isn't true: Not seeming to feel pain doesn't mean you *aren't* in pain. Stoicism aside, some studies of anesthesia suggest that you might be in pain even if you don't seem to be, from the inside, to yourself. I often have dreams that I'm in pain. There's a particularly unpleasant recurring one that some kind of wild, unruly animal, like a jungle cat or a rabid dog, is biting or mauling me. In the dream, it truly hurts, but then I wake up, and I'm in no pain. This almost feels like an exception to Strawson's rule, a case of seeming to feel pain without feeling pain, of completely illusory pain, like when I dream that I'm mad at my husband, and the most white-hot anger dissolves upon waking—he's done nothing wrong. My mind has conjured up pain like an emotion. Out of what? On the other hand, Daniel Dennett describes "the painfulness of pain," any and all pain, as "sheer illusion." (In this view there is no conscious pain, or indeed conscious anything.)

On the first page of *The Worst of Evils*, Dormandy writes:

In times past sleep, joy, hope, happiness and relief from physical pain were part of the same package, a blessing that the gods of Mount Olympus (or wherever)

occasionally bestowed on mortals. The idea that any part
of this bounty could be separated from the rest would
not have been understood . . . The Persian physician
Abu Ali al-Hussayn ibn 'Abdallah ibn Sina revered in
Christian Europe for centuries as Avicenna, laid down
that potions must accomplish three things. They must
alleviate pain. They must calm the mind. And they must
induce restful sleep.

Dormandy then adds, "Physical pain is of course still
perceived as being related to sleeplessness." An equa-
tion of consciousness with pain. Would that mean that
painlessness—happiness—and unconsciousness are the
same? That to be aware is to be unhappy?

A man I know has an exceedingly rare affliction—so rare
and strange he's been written up in neurology journals.
One night in his life, he went to sleep, but didn't. He had
one of those nights, in his own words, "after which one
feels one has not slept at all," not in itself an unfamiliar
experience—but the next night it happened again, and
every night afterward, it continued to happen. It was not
the condition known as "paradoxical insomnia," where
patients insist they aren't sleeping, despite evidence to the
contrary, which inevitably turns up in their sleep studies.
"I can only imagine that if you have the subjective experience of struggle," my friend writes, "being told that you
aren't struggling at all must be maddening. But at least the

data offers some clarification. *Look*, says the technician, *you are simply wrong.*" For these unfortunate people, to seem to have insomnia is not to have insomnia.

My friend's case is different. He knows when he's asleep, but it feels as though he's awake while he's sleeping. His brain waves go through sleep-like patterns, and yet he remains, on some level, alert: conscious sleeping. He says that people always ask him if he's sleepy. "No," he answers, "I'm not sleepy. Were I failing to sleep, I would be dead. I sleep perfectly well. What I cannot do is cease being aware, and so what I am is *tired*." An excess of awareness is a burden on the body. The Spanish writer Javier Marías once wrote that he always felt exhausted after getting off a plane, due to his fear of flying—these flights "could be relied upon to transform me into a highly superstitious little boy, who reached his various destinations feeling utterly drained after the hours of tension and the indescribable effort of having to 'carry' the plane." He felt appalled by his "excessively relaxed" fellow passengers doing nothing to help the flight, as he himself was devoted to "controlling" and "protecting" it.

I've always had occasional insomnia. It's the same type as my mother's—we fall asleep easily, but wake up in the early-morning hours, between three and five, to worry and plan, to worry over plans, to "carry the plane." Sometimes I stay in bed until I fall back asleep, a fitful desperate hour of rest before my alarm goes off; other times I see the sun come through the blinds and give up trying, and I get up and make extra coffee. There's the consoling possibility of an afternoon nap; because I live in the Mountain Time Zone but work on Eastern time, I can stop working around 3:00 p.m. if I need to, and doze for an hour on the couch. It's consoling even though I usually don't do it, like a sleeping pill you keep on hand but rarely resort to taking. Instead, I drag myself to the gym and try to go to bed early.

Recently, for a few weeks, my insomnia suddenly changed forms. I still woke up early, but I also had a lot of trouble falling asleep—both at night and whenever I'd try to make up the loss with a nap. I'd lie there and just couldn't relax—feeling frantic and panicky and weepy, like a toddler a parent calls "overtired." I became convinced it was a permanent change: that I would never sleep normally again, that I'd simply forgotten how to fall asleep. (I was wrong about that; I took a week off from work and recovered.)

During this wretched period, I became obsessed with Emil Cioran's obsession with insomnia. I had read more than once the Romanian philosopher's line about "the importance of insomnia": "The importance of insomnia is so colossal that I am tempted to define man as the animal who cannot sleep." Cioran is a writer I'm always drawn to in quotation but find kind of unreadable at length. But I went searching for the context of this sentence, and found a beautiful essay called "Cioran's Insomnia" by Willis G. Regier, originally published in *Modern Language Notes*. Regier writes that Cioran "considered his insomnia to be 'the greatest experience' of his life." The word "greatest" here is probably irreducibly ambiguous; he may have meant not "most wonderful" but largest, most overwhelming; however, he seemed to cherish his insomnia too—it was self-defining. "When I was twenty I stopped sleeping and I consider that the grandest tragedy," Cioran wrote. He started, allowed, or cultivated rumors that he didn't sleep at all for fifty years, a medical impossibility. This "insistence on wearing his pajamas as a hair shirt," as Adam Gopnik once put it, was "irresistible." Rereading this now, I think Gopnik must have been saying that the claim was irresistible to Cioran. But I initially thought he meant the quality was irresistible in general; it certainly makes Cioran irresistible to me. (I almost called this essay "The Importance of Insomnia.")

Regier collects and catalogs Cioran's many thoughts on insomnia: "Insomnia is a form of heroism because it transforms each new day into a combat lost in advance"; "To save the word 'grandeur' from officialdom, we should use it only apropos of insomnia or heresy"; "On the heights of despair, nobody has the right to sleep." (*On the Heights of Despair* is Cioran's book about "madness and death, the absurdity of existence, and the agony of consciousness," as the Google Books copy tells it. A user review quoted on the same page says, "The adolescent despair on display here charmed me for a while, but by the end of the (quite short) book I was getting tired of it." Another says, "What a waste of a good prose style! . . . I've been through too much suffering to be a nihilist anymore.") More Cioran: "To keep the mind vigilant, there is only coffee, disease, insomnia, or the obsession of death"; "These hours I am so conscious of I am wresting from nothingness . . . If I were asleep they would never have belonged to me, they would never even have existed." (He treasures the time, painful though it may be, rescued from sleep, the way we treasure our painful memories for their intensity.) And on how to fall asleep: "You must dismiss every impulse of thought, any shadow of an idea. For it is the formulated idea, the distinct idea, that is sleep's worst enemy." My own remedies for insomnia all entail tricking myself out of thinking clearly. In one version, I try to turn my brain into a random-number generator, silently sounding out three-digit numbers in no particular order: *One-zero-nine. Five-five-seven. Three-forty-two.* (Dormandy writes that "a knock-out blow was one of the earliest methods of anesthesia"—one cure for pain is to be distracted by other pain.)

Cioran also wrote, "The desire to die was my one and only concern; to it I have sacrificed everything, even death." He spoke of "the voluptuousness of suffering." In *The Trouble with Being Born* (all his books have perfect titles), he wrote, "It is not worth the bother of killing yourself, since you always kill yourself too late." He wrote another book called *The Temptation to Exist.* Like many suicidally depressed people, he believed in the consoling possibility of suicide. See what my friend Martin once called "Nietzsche's zinger": "The thought of suicide is a great consolation: by means of it one gets through many a dark night." It's the suffering insomniac's nuclear option, the ultimate untaken sleeping pill.

Pain and insomnia have become inextricable in my mind. If we leave out those awful few weeks when I could barely sleep at all, my insomnia is nothing compared to my husband's. John cannot (just *can not*) fall asleep without chemical assistance, without taking a strong benzodiazepine. It wasn't always so, though he never slept easily. It's gotten worse as his tinnitus has gotten worse. Sometimes he tries to explain how bad it is to me. "You wouldn't believe how loud it is," he says. "It's SO LOUD." I can't and don't want to imagine the volume. Sometimes he tries to explain the noise's character. He found a bit of a video—the soundtrack from a horror movie, I think—whose crackling, unsettling static seemed to approximate the horror in his ears. He played it with the volume up high, and I felt deeply uncomfortable. He tried to increase the immersive reality, by having me listen with headphones, even louder—to make the sound private. I almost let him do this, but then I refused. I didn't want to know, I had to admit to myself and to him. I can't bear to understand, that fully, his pain. And I do think it's pain, though unlike regular pain it can't be treated, it can't be killed, even if the ear dies; the auditory cortex, lacking input, keeps creating the static, the aural equivalent of phantom pain. And I always think pain in your head—a migraine, a scratched cornea, an earache—is worse than pain that's farther away, in your fingers or your ankle. It feels more inescapable. It's too close to your mind.

Once, in an interview, the poet Sandra Simonds was asked, "What is your idea of happiness?" She responded,

"Happiness is basically irrelevant to my life. I am not even convinced happiness is ethical." I think about this all the time. Does anyone deserve to be happy? The Swedish researcher Carl Cederström believes our current "happiness fantasy," the delusion that we should or even can be happy, is based on something like personal fulfillment and "pursuing an authentic life." But we look to cultural norms to tell us what is "authentic"—as though "good taste" were happiness. Cederström has also said, "It's impossible to actually know what happiness is."

In *The Happiness Myth*, Jennifer Michael Hecht argues that "the basic modern assumptions about how to be happy are nonsense." Euphoria is one form of happiness, but "we devalue euphoria in our drugs . . . because we value productivity." Coffee and antidepressants are good drugs, or moral drugs, because they don't prevent us from doing our jobs. But opiates and alcohol are morally questionable— they change reality too much. They're also addictive, you might argue, but so are coffee and antidepressants. And so what? Dormandy quotes from "a popular and practical British textbook" for medical students that advises "analgesics should be given to control pain but without leading to undue dependence or addiction." "But how could dependence and addiction be avoided?" Dormandy asks. "And why should it be?" Yes, why? If something makes us feel better, quiets our pain, why shouldn't we do it? Because it might shorten our life span? Again, I find Dormandy clarifying: "Every extension of the human life-span tends to increase the sum total of human suffering." I don't want to die of liver failure, but I don't want to live forever either, and as my father often says, you have to die of something.

"Happiness" is not well defined. In addition to euphoria, Hecht points out, the word can mean "a good day" or "a happy life." These different kinds of happiness "are often at odds." Too many good days (weekends or vacation days, for most people) could prevent you from having a happy (long, fulfilling, stable) life. But "modern expert advice is hopelessly devoted to 'happy life' happiness," Hecht writes, at the expense of euphoric moments or simple happy days. It's a question of perspective, or perhaps resolution—how zoomed in you are when examining your life. How will you know, on your deathbed, if you were happy? Will you consider the gestalt, the overall average of happiness, or one peak if exquisitely brief experience? (Is it possible not to know if you are happy? Is this something people question? I've not lain on that bed.)

Toward the end of her life, in a letter to her friend Ruth, Sylvia Plath wrote, "When I was 'happy' domestically I felt a gag in my throat. Now that my domestic life, until I get a permanent live-in girl, is chaos, I am living like a Spartan, writing through huge fevers and producing free stuff I had locked in me for years. I feel astounded and very lucky." The happiness of unhappiness! I think sometimes that sadness, pain, and even suffering are part of happiness, that sadness and happiness are somehow alike. Shortly after reading these sentences of Plath's, quoted in Janet Malcolm's *The Silent Woman*, I read this line about a character, a child, in the novel *Outline* by Rachel Cusk:

"For the first time in his life he experienced cruelty, and along with it certain new kinds of unhappiness: loneliness, homesickness, the longing for his mother and father." Rather, I should say, I misread this line—as "new kinds of happiness." It made sense to me that way. Loneliness and longing and nostalgia do feel sometimes like varieties of happiness, like something to indulge in, like when I read old emails on purpose to make myself miss someone.

Dormandy's book includes a reproduction of a photograph of Gian Lorenzo Bernini's *The Ecstasy of Saint Teresa*. The photo is confusing—it's a photo of a sculpture, a close-up of her head, but it looks like a painting. Dormandy's caption admits that the baroque work "has repelled many," but, he writes, "no other work of art so brilliantly conveys the ecstasy of pain . . . St Theresa herself spoke of the experience of the angel piercing her heart as an indescribable mixture of torture and joy." According to an art site called The Archive for Research in Archetypal Symbolism, the "erotic intensity" of Saint Teresa's vision is suggested by her "swooning expression and languid pose," while the "deep folds of drapery" "convey her agitation."

Never mind how drapery conveys agitation; this reminds me of the sex dreams women have under anesthesia. These fantasias might serve as a distraction, the mind's way of letting you leave your pain ("ecstasy" meaning "to stand outside," as in, to be beside yourself; an out-of-body experience). Knocked-out patients sometimes cry during surgery—it's called "lacrimation" or "the abreaction," usually seen as unrelated to conscious tears. But maybe it is just the trauma of surgery. Anne Boyer once spoke of her uncontrollable weeping after chemotherapy, an experience that almost wasn't hers: "The body has its own automatic suffering." Pain makes you cry; crying releases endorphins, the body's off-brand morphine; therefore, pain feels good. But what of the theory that the memory of pain is worse than pain, which seems related to the idea that the fear of pain is effectively pain? Sufficiently keen anticipation of pain *hurts*.

My own past suffering is often a great source of comfort to me. This must mean I've never really suffered.

2018

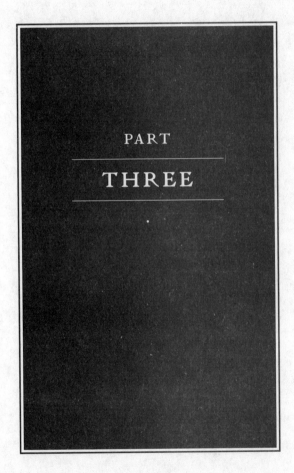

PART

THREE

TRUE CRIME

One long weekend in mid-October 2016, John and I met three friends from D.C. in Albuquerque for the annual Balloon Fiesta. We ate green chile at every meal; we gawked at the hot-air balloons shaped like dragons and elephants and the Bimbo Bear; we burned off our altitude hangovers in the afternoons watching *Ink Master* at our Airbnb.

We also talked incessantly about the election, and our addiction to the news. We checked the news on our phones while we talked. We rage-bonded over our hatred of the purists who claimed that, given the options, they weren't going to vote at all. So harmonious was our accord, we regretted we'd be unable to watch the upcoming debates together. One morning, standing in line at the fairgrounds for piñon coffee, our friend A said she wasn't sure what she would do with herself after the election. Despite our worst fears, we still assumed Hillary would pull through in the end. We believed in "the end." We believed the glut of news could not possibly last. She said, "I think I'll almost miss it."

I remembered A's comment on "Indictment Day," as the media or regular people (I'm not sure who got to it first) dubbed October 30, 2017, when Robert Mueller filed the first indictments in his investigation into the Trump campaign's involvement with Russia. My friend M, who had also been with us that weekend in New Mexico, sent me a text that evening: "Read the news for like six hours today, feel almost hungover." I'd done the same, and it was unsatisfying; I didn't know how to feel. Was the news truly good—a sign of good things to come—or seemingly good, but actually bad? I no longer trusted the news to tell me, or myself to know the difference. I felt I had lost the thread.

I watched Indictment Day happen without feeling involved. It was like being at a party when you're not in the mood. But I could see that my friends were getting some kind of high from it. Wanting to take part in that, I kept clicking links. From my unsure remove, I could tell they were experiencing something close to what I experienced on January 10, 2017, the day the infamous "pee tape" dossier was published by BuzzFeed—I was so absorbed in Twitter that evening, we were late to an event—and before that, on October 7, 2016, the day the *Access Hollywood* tape got out (the tape of Trump saying "I moved on her like a bitch . . . I just start kissing them. It's like a magnet . . . And when you're a star, they let you do it. You can do anything . . . Grab 'em by the pussy"). I was on a train when that news dropped, and I didn't take my eyes off my phone for the two-hour trip. I gorged on the news like I was starving. And I could see, via Twitter, that my friends were doing it too. It was hitting all the same pleasure centers as watching TV— in both the old way, where everyone watches the same shows at the same time, and the new way, where streaming makes it possible to binge unto sickness. What we felt was close to joy, an intercity orgy of communal schadenfreude.

I wanted that joy on Indictment Day, but I wasn't getting it. In the past, bad news for Trump had necessarily felt like good news for me, but I was getting used to my vindictive hopes being disappointed. I kept checking the news every twenty minutes anyway. It was comically like real addiction: My brain had adapted to high doses of news, and I needed more and more news just to feel something. But quantity wasn't the problem. I wanted to know what it *meant*. There were the usual let's-be-clear, make-no-mistake takes in abundance, the reviews of the news, but I didn't trust them. They contradicted one another; they rang false. I trusted only the dry news, the fact-checked reportage without overtly apparent bias, that didn't tell me how to feel, that I couldn't even really understand. The narrative-making meta-media had betrayed me.

"When the first American newspaper, Benjamin Harris's *Publick Occurences Both Forreign and Domestick*, appeared in Boston on September 25, 1690, it promised to furnish news regularly once a month." This rather hilarious fact is from the historian Daniel Boorstin's *The Image*, published in 1962. Boorstin goes on to explain how inventions like photography, the phonograph, radio, and motion pictures, proliferating rapidly between the late 1800s and early 1900s, gave "new meaning" to "verisimilitude," increasing demand for images and recordings from life. Before long we had "round-the-clock media":

> The news gap became so narrow that in order to have additional "news" for each new edition or each new broadcast it was necessary to plan in advance the stages by which any available news would be unveiled. After the weekly and the daily came the "extras" and the numerous regular editions. The Philadelphia *Evening Bulletin* soon had seven editions a day. No rest for the newsman. With more space to fill, he had to fill it ever more quickly. In order to justify the numerous editions, it was increasingly necessary that the news constantly change or at least seem to change.

The news, in this model, is not something reported (retold after the fact) but something created (planned out before the fact).

According to Boorstin, it became "financially necessary" for the media, after building this machine, to keep it running. The costs of printing and broadcasting were high; constant content kept the money flowing back in. They accomplished this by creating "pseudo-events," or seemingly newsworthy, reportable happenings to fill pages and airtime. He gives as an example a televised parade to celebrate the return of General Douglas MacArthur from Korea in 1951. The event was engineered to look good on TV, with "cameras carefully focused on 'significant' happenings—that is, those which emphasized the drama of the occasion." They recorded "wild cheering and enthusiastic crowds"—but this cheering was more a response to the cameras, the idea of being on TV, than it was to MacArthur. (It's like that scene in *Grease* when the kids at the dance, after being told to act natural and avoid the camera, all wave and blow kisses at it.) Anyone who wasn't near a camera felt bored and disappointed. The result was that people who attended the live parade experienced inverted FOMO (fear of missing out): "We should have stayed at home and watched it on TV."

A political debate is another good example of a pseudoevent. In a previous life (a previous decade), I rarely watched the news, but I married a man who follows politics like sports—watching news clips like replays, rooting for his team. In 2016, I got sucked into watching every single debate from the primaries on. There were nights when I wasn't in the mood, but if I tried to leave the room, I'd still hear the debates playing across the apartment, which distracted me from reading, and Twitter offered no alternative distraction. So I'd join in the "fun"—I'd watch with Twitter open. Debates, like the news, give us something to tweet about. It's fodder for jokes; it's material.

It's strange how our memories get so rooted in place. When I was a kid, I understood the assassination of JFK to be the single moment of my parents' lives that was so significant they were supposed to remember where they were when it happened. But I have so many moments like that, just from the past year, often in the same few hundred square feet: I was on the couch during the debates. I was on the couch when we watched the election results. (I had been at a friend's house, a party of sorts, until I couldn't stand it and came home.) I was at my desk the next morning, on Valium and crying, when I saw tweets about Hillary's concession speech. (I could not stand to watch it.) I was at my desk during Obama's last press conference. I was in the armchair when the dossier came out. At my desk for Indictment Day.

My memories of these comparatively trivial moments, in the prickliness of their detail, have the quality of memories of large-scale disaster. I think about them the way I think about 9/11, which I experienced from afar, on TV. Horrifying, but removed—not traumatic in the way that a car crash is traumatic, or that 9/11 would have been had I lived in New York at the time. What nags me about these memories, these unhappy memories, is that I think that I think of them fondly.

For years, I've believed there are two kinds of happiness. On the one hand, there's the happiness of stability: a good job, a loving family, dependable American-dream prosperity. On the other, there's the happiness of intense experience: dizzying highs and crushing lows in quick succession. My theory is that when we're young, we prefer the second kind of happiness; we take a lot of risks because the lows improve the highs. As we get older, as the pressures of conformity increase and the lows take their toll, we strive for the first kind of happiness. But we continue to prefer our painful memories—stable life may be happier, but unstable life is more interesting. It's as though being happy on a day-to-day basis doesn't make us happy overall.

Believing this scares me, as much as the news scares me. I worry that, despite the wages of stress on my body—my blood pressure is higher, my gums are receding—I'll look back on this whole awful year with *nostalgia*. "Nostalgia," etymologically, means "homesickness" or "return-home pain"—again, the significance of place. I also find that the "pain" part of the word (*algos*, as in fibromyalgia), the longing part, bleeds over into the "return-home" part—I'm not just nostalgic for my past; I'm nostalgic for my pain. My own past suffering can be a great source of comfort. Why is that? Because it's over? Or because it's a badge of honor?

If we treat the news like sports, like a hobby, a dramatic "season" is more fun, even when some of that fun feels like pain. The disappointment of the losses makes the glory of the wins that much better. When I think of "fun" news days like Indictment Day, which couldn't have occurred without the horror of Election Day, it's like there's another me to watch me in my pain, a spectator to the drama.

My media tastes have gotten weird this year, weird for me. There are things I can't stomach anymore—I never listen to NPR in the car now. I've replaced it with top-forty stations; vacuity seems preferable to pandering. My "guilty pleasures" are different. I watch a lot of horror movies, really wanting to be terrified. Artificial horror displaces actual horror, for a couple of hours at least, though nothing is ever scary enough. I've started reading true crime: all the lurid reality porn of the news, but with pain-relieving distance. In true crime we already know how it ends.

I picked up a copy of *In Cold Blood*, which I'd never read before, when I saw it on my library's rack of recently returned books. (I love the randomness of this shelf; it's like anti-curation, like Oulipo.) It was so good I didn't want to read it; I'd read ten or twenty pages and then put it down and look for something worse to read instead. I either wanted to save it for my future self or didn't believe I deserved it. I mentioned this on Twitter, and several people, perhaps thinking it was journalistic ethics I was interested in rather than crime, recommended *The Journalist and the Murderer* by Janet Malcolm, quoting its famous first sentence: "Every journalist who is not too stupid or too full of himself to notice what is going on knows that what he does is morally indefensible." My interest was piqued. I was feeling like the media had fucked up—it fucked up in its coverage of the election and the candidates, and in so doing had fucked up history for all time and my life personally. Vindictively, maybe, I thought a screed against the morals of journalists sounded pretty good. So I read that next.

The Journalist and the Murderer is about Jeffrey Mac-Donald, convicted in 1979 of killing his pregnant wife and two daughters nine years earlier, and Joe McGinniss, who wrote a bestselling book about MacDonald called *Fatal*

Vision in 1983. MacDonald, a Green Beret, was originally cleared of guilt by a military hearing but arrested years later. He has always maintained his innocence—he claims to this day that a group of four hippies broke into the house and attacked them, Manson Family–style, chanting "Acid is groovy" and "Kill the pigs," wounding him but leaving him alive.

MacDonald contracted McGinniss (who'd earned celebrity status from the success of his first book, *The Selling of the President 1968*, about the Nixon campaign) to tell his story and clear his name. McGinniss was added to MacDonald's defense team and given full access; the "journalist" and the "murderer" became friends. However, through the course of the trial, McGinniss came to believe that MacDonald was guilty. They continued corresponding after MacDonald went to prison, but McGinniss refused to show him the manuscript before it was published—at which point MacDonald was shocked to discover his friend had written a portrait of a killer. He sued McGinniss for breach of contract.

Malcolm takes this second case, the civil suit, as occasion to meditate on the relationship between author and subject. Why, we may wonder, did MacDonald trust McGinniss to be his advocate, when McGinniss had pulled an inside-job switcheroo once before? Nixon's team had invited McGinniss along for the ride, and then he exposed them. Don't journalists always have an agenda, and isn't their loyalty to the agenda first? Shouldn't we treat them like vampires—never invite them inside?

But "something seems to happen to people when they

meet a journalist," Malcolm observes, "and what happens is exactly the opposite of what one would expect": "One would think that extreme wariness and caution would be the order of the day, but in fact childish trust and impetuosity are far more common." Even more dangerous, perhaps, the journalistic subject "lives in fear of being found uninteresting, and many of the strange things that subjects say to writers—things of almost suicidal rashness— they say out of their desperate need to keep the writer's attention riveted." This makes me think of the way Twitter allows us to converse directly with journalists. Though most of us won't get the chance to play the subject, following a journalist creates a false intimacy. It encourages that same blind trust, which the journalist is then poised to exploit. Like the relationship between journalist and subject, the relationship between newsmaker and news consumer is mutually parasitic.

Malcolm takes a strong dislike to McGinniss, who does not come out looking well in the trial. Though he never promised to let MacDonald dictate the story of the book, his letters to MacDonald are painfully misleading:

> There could not be a worse nightmare than the one you are living through now—but it is only a phase. Total strangers can recognize within five minutes that you did not receive a fair trial . . . It's a hell of a thing—spend the summer making a new friend and then the bastards come along and lock him up. But not for long, Jeffrey—not for long.

He continues this way for years, discouraging Mac-
Donald from communicating with other writers who
show interest in covering the case, plying him for more
background. MacDonald records and sends him a series
of tapes, essentially narrating his life story. Malcolm gets
copies of these too (she finds them banal), plus heaps of
other evidence related to the murder—MacDonald seems
to trust her as well, though at this point—in prison on three
consecutive life sentences—I suppose he has less to lose.
She opts not, however, to review all this material; she feels
"oppressed" by this "mountain of documents":

> I have read little of the material he sent—trial transcripts,
> motions, declarations, affidavits, reports. A document ar-
> rives, I glance at it, see words like "bloody syringe," "blue
> threads," "left chest puncture," "unidentified finger-
> prints," "Kimberly's urine," and add it to the pile. I know
> I cannot learn anything about MacDonald's guilt or in-
> nocence from this material. It is like looking for proof or
> disproof of God in a flower—it all depends on how you
> read the evidence.

The facts, she suggests, can be made to mean one
thing, or its exact opposite. Whether it's piles of evidence
or piles of news, you read it through the lens of whatever
conclusion you've already come to, and once you've come
to a conclusion, it's extremely uncomfortable to change
your mind.

In his 2012 book, *A Wilderness of Error*, the documentary filmmaker Errol Morris objects to Malcolm's position: "It comes down to an issue of truth . . . And yes, there is such a thing. There is a fact of the matter of whether you killed your family or you didn't. It's not just somehow thinking makes it so." This is taken from a transcript of an interview between Morris and MacDonald. Morris has taken MacDonald's side: The book argues that MacDonald is, if not innocent, at least not guilty. "There's a difference," Morris says—"guilty," in the eyes of the law, means "beyond a reasonable doubt." If there's reasonable doubt, then you're *not guilty* even if you actually did it. Real life is not like fiction, he writes, not like *The Count of Monte Cristo*, in which "all the pieces can be engineered to fit perfectly together." He goes on, "Reality is different. We have to discover what is out there—what is real and what is merely a product of our imagination."

Malcolm's book is remarkably self-aware; she cops to the same pitfalls of journalism that she criticizes. In writing the book, she willingly steps into that "morally indefensible" author-subject relation. She notes the parallels between her own correspondence with MacDonald and McGinniss's: "I was no less enamored of the sound of my voice than McGinniss had been of his." But Morris seems unaware of the ways in which he manipulates the evidence to serve his own ends. Having succeeded once before, with the film *The Thin Blue Line*, in getting a man out of prison and off death row (a man who'd been wrongly accused and convicted in Texas of killing a cop), Morris is out to play hero again, to play Henry Fonda's role in *Twelve Angry Men*. *A Wilderness of Error*, at five hundred–plus pages that include diagrams and other images of court-admitted evidence, has a veneer of comprehensiveness, of objectivity. But Morris tends to skim over or elide any evidence that would implicate MacDonald, interfering with his narrative of wrongful conviction.

For example, *Fatal Vision* recounts a story McGinniss heard from a friend and former lover of MacDonald's (he had encouraged McGinniss to speak to her). She says that MacDonald once dangled her ten-year-old son over the edge of a dock, "threatening to drop him head first into the water," and then later exploded in anger toward him on a boat trip and threatened to "crush his skull." McGinniss then calls the son, in college now, who says he remembers the incident "with real terror to this day" and reports that MacDonald actually threw him off the side of the boat.

Morris doesn't question the relevance of this anecdote; he just doesn't mention it. Instead, he repeatedly questions the validity of the theory that MacDonald is a "psychopath" or that psychopathy even exists ("People, suddenly and without warning, are not transformed into monsters"). This was one of the revelations of *The Thin Blue Line*, that psychopathy is circular—we say he did it because he's a psychopath, but if he didn't do it, how would we know he's a psychopath? And maybe psychopathy *doesn't* exist. Malcolm is also suspicious of the magical explanatory power of the diagnosis: "The concept of the psychopath is in fact an admission of failure to solve the mystery of evil— it is merely a restatement of the mystery."

But don't people sometimes, suddenly and without warning, commit horrible crimes? I think of Lowell Lee Andrews, "the nicest boy in Wolcott," who was on death row at the same time as Perry Smith and Dick Hickock from *In Cold Blood* for murdering his parents and sister. Andrews tried to make the crime look like a break-in—in a parallel to MacDonald's version of events—and the police found him sitting on the porch, apparently unperturbed. (Nonchalance didn't serve MacDonald either; his blasé appearance on *The Dick Cavett Show* enraged his father-in-law, triggering a series of events that led to his eventual arrest.)

Throughout his account, Morris gives credence to secondary evidence like psychiatric assessments and polygraph tests only when they support his own theory, and he fails to address the inconsistencies in MacDonald's story. Morris's journalistic agenda is clear. Nevertheless, he does succeed in making a case for the trial as a miscarriage of justice. He convinced me that the investigators mishandled evidence and failed to properly secure the crime scene. This, along with the existence of at least one other suspect without an alibi, introduces room for reasonable doubt. However, all MacDonald's appeals have been denied, and by maintaining his innocence, he has relinquished the possibility of parole.

I have not read *Fatal Vision*, which by virtue of coming first has become the official story on the MacDonald murders. I have not reviewed the mountain of evidence, like Morris or his research assistant, whom he thanks for becoming an encyclopedic resource on the case. But you can probably tell that I lean toward believing MacDonald is guilty. I am not entirely sure why. I knew nothing about the case before reading *The Journalist and the Murderer*, and while Malcolm withholds judgment on the matter, she gives the impression of presuming MacDonald's innocence if only to spite the hated McGinniss. I like to think I came to Morris's book with an open mind, but within a few pages, I could see the seams of his rhetoric. His aims may be noble, but his tactics are shady. I began to distrust him, and then almost as a matter of course, I found myself siding against MacDonald, *rooting* against him. It gave me a reason to finish the book: the search for holes in Morris's argument. I could not read it in the spirit of "negative capability"— Keats's phrase for the state "when a man is capable of being in uncertainties, mysteries, doubts, without any irritable reaching after fact and reason"—any more than Morris could write the book in that spirit.

Was there something sick about reading the book in this way, needing to discredit it? I was reminded of those disheartening studies on confirmation bias, showing challenges to a person's prior beliefs tend only to strengthen those beliefs. If Morris was rejecting the "facts" that didn't jibe with his agenda, so was I. I had a similar feeling when Donna Brazile's book *Hacks: The Inside Story* came out and her claim that Hillary Clinton had "rigged" the Democratic primary made the rounds. I did not even read these stories; my immediate reaction was refusal, refusal to accept another story in the media of Hillary's corruption. Not long afterward, there was a round of corrections; Brazile had misread a memo about the general election, believing it applied to the primary. But Elizabeth Warren was already on record lending support to Brazile's claim, and then we got corrections of the corrections—*here's why the primary really was rigged, if you think about it.* The meta-corrections were more about the corruption of party politics and campaign money in general, but Hillary's name was still attached; the first version of the story has a tendency to stick.

In the era of fake news—a natural extension of the era of news proper—we don't just look to the media for facts, we look to it for narratives. And with plenty of news to choose from (we can't read it all), we naturally gravitate toward the news and news sources that align with our existing worldview, our ongoing narrative. Journalists must know this; they must, consciously or not, play to our desires by oversimplifying stories—ignoring facts that compromise the greater narrative—or only pursuing stories that they perceive to fit an existing and popular narrative in the first place. This is how it becomes parasitic: We need the drugs, and they need us to buy them.

Reporters jump on a story that fits the "Hillary = bad" narrative because it makes people emotional; it's guaranteed to spread on social media. True or not, people will read and share that story because they want it to be true. As Kevin Young writes in *Bunk*, speaking of the "Great Moon Hoax" of 1835, when *The Sun* published a series of articles claiming that the (real) astronomer Sir John Herschel had observed bat-like humanoids on the moon, "The story seemed too good, if not to be true then not to be told." *The Sun* was penny-press trash, but does the appeal of a sure-fire hit make even legitimate outlets cut corners on fact-checking? It certainly seems to—they're ad-supported, not sponsored by patrons as newspapers once were. Traffic, not just truth, keeps newspapers alive.

When we talk about the ethics of journalism, we're usually talking about the ethics of producing it. But what about the ethics of consuming the news? We can't put all the blame on the media for creating these narratives, these pseudo-events. As Boorstin writes:

> This world of ambiguity . . . is not created by demagogues or crooks, by conspiracy or evil purpose. The efficient mass production of pseudo-events—in all kinds of packages, in black and white, in technicolor, in words, and in a thousand other forms—is the work of the whole machinery of our society. It is the daily product of men of good will.

In a piece called "Information, Technology, and the Virtues of Ignorance," originally published in *Daedalus* in

1986, Daniel Dennett questions whether information technology is "poised to *ruin our lives*" (the emphases, here and below, are Dennett's). Dennett says that people all want to lead "good lives" in two senses: "We want to lead lives that are interesting, exciting, fulfilling, and happy, and we want to lead lives that are morally good." Increasingly, however, access to information will make this difficult, if not impossible—we will have to choose between happiness and morality. Our ancestors were

> *capable* of living lives of virtue . . . a virtue that *depended on* unavoidable ignorance. Modern technology has robbed us of the sorts of virtue that depend on such ignorance, for ignorance is all too avoidable today. Information technology has multiplied our *opportunities to know,* and our traditional ethical doctrines overwhelm us by turning these opportunities into newfound *obligations to know.*

Thirty years later, this theory, or prophecy, feels grimly true. I do not know how to live an ethical life, when I consider the implications of almost every aspect of my existence—on the rest of the world, on future generations. I know what it means that I eat meat whenever I want, that I work in advertising, that I fly many times per year, that I'm psychologically dependent on a device that was built under sweatshop conditions. When it breaks, or just gets slow and inconvenient, I'll buy another. I know because I read the news, and I keep doing it all anyway.

2017

I'M SO TIRED

In April 2018, a woman calling herself "Apathetic Idealist" wrote a letter to Roxane Gay's advice column in *The New York Times*, asking for help overcoming a sense of political apathy—a newly acquired "condition of paralysis" that was keeping her from engaging in "real action." This condition began in November 2016, when Donald Trump won the U.S. presidential election. "I continue to be outraged by this administration's treatment of Latinos, Native Americans, Muslims, L.G.B.T. folks, women and so many others," she writes. "But I'm struggling to summon a response."

"I have no doubt that many people can relate to your letter. I can relate to it," Gay's response begins. She continues: "It is damn hard to expand the limits of our empathy when our emotional attention is already stretched too thin."

I can relate too. For the past several months, I've experienced a creeping psychic exhaustion. "I'm in a numb period," I tell my friends when they send me frantic texts about the day's news. My emotions seem blocked.

In a way, that comes as a relief. The news doesn't leave me incapacitated; I acknowledge the horror and move on. But the numbness has other, unexpected effects. On the mild end, it's harder to be interesting. My conversation is more boring. I also have less empathy available, even for my family. Recently, John and I were in Boston for a week. I was working at my company's office, and he had spent the day doing research in Harvard's library; in the evening, he boarded a crowded rush-hour train, en route to meet me at our downtown hotel. From there we planned to find somewhere to eat al fresco. As he was exiting the train, someone stepped on his toe with so much force that the nail was partially detached and partially driven into the nail bed. He arrived at the hotel room with a shoe full of blood.

There's a reason "denailing" is used as a method of torture. John's best friend is in training to become an emergency medical technician, and the two of them had talked about the pain scale just a few days before. "I'm at about an eight," John said to the nurse on staff at the urgent care facility. This is in the "severe" range, with ten being the worst possible pain. According to one version of the pain scale, eight translates to "utterly horrible": "pain so intense you can no longer think clearly at all." In the eight-to-ten range (ten is "unimaginable, unspeakable"), if the pain goes on for a long time, "suicide is frequently contemplated." I don't think John was exaggerating; he was actually writhing. The pain seemed to be coming in excruciating waves. As we waited over two hours to see a doctor, I rubbed his shoulder and let him crush my hand. The pain was awful to witness, but I knew once he was treated he'd be fine; it was just a toe. I felt irritable, impatient. Hungry.

I stepped out of the waiting room to call my father, an internist; I find his calm voice and clinical terminology comforting in a medical emergency. I started to tell him what had happened and was surprised to hear my voice break. Why was *I* crying? It didn't feel like a rush of sympathy. It felt selfish and indulgent, as though the accident had happened to me. A malfunction of emotion.

I'm in the habit of searching and rereading my old tweets—I tweet every day, so they're the closest thing I have to a diary. Looking back through my timeline, I see that on almost any given day in 2016 or 2017, I was responding to the news. There was real rage and terror in these tweets. I was angry about the news and angry about the response, the constant thought-terminating clichés of *This is not normal* and *Let that sink in* and *Stay mad*. "How hard is it to 'stay mad'?" I tweeted on March 20, 2017. "Just watch 20 seconds of any news clip at all."

In early 2017, John printed out the phone numbers of our local representatives and stuck them on the fridge. We started calling them weekly, demanding, even begging them to fight on our behalf—to fight the dismantling of the Affordable Care Act and the Americans with Disabilities Act, to fight the attacks on minorities and immigrants and trans people, to fight for gun control. My heart would beat faster as I made these calls, trying to translate my anger and fear into something coherent.

Sometimes the public outcry seemed to work. A rushed Republican bill to repeal and replace the ACA—a flawed but important step toward universal health care, established under President Obama—failed to find support. It felt like a victory. But a few months later, those same senators cut billions from government health care programs like Medicare under the guise of "tax reform." I made a number of calls to my reps about the tax plan, but it didn't help; this time, they had the votes.

I haven't called my senators in months. It was starting to feel like a waste of time and energy. Most of the time, our Republican senator's office doesn't even answer the phone. Most of the time, outrage itself feels largely useless. It did, in fact, get hard to stay mad. The news is still horrifying, at home and around the world; I know this intellectually, but the physical feeling of horror is gone. Keeping up with the war in Syria, refugee crises, or melting sea ice is almost necessarily an exercise in acceptance—these are situations that are getting worse.

There's a name for this feeling: "compassion fatigue." The term is not very common today, but it had a cultural moment. In 2000, it even made its way into a *New Yorker* cartoon: Two men in suits have just passed a disgruntled-looking homeless man on the ground; one suit says to the other, "Here I was, all this time, worrying that maybe I'm a selfish person, and now it turns out I've been suffering from compassion fatigue."

According to a Google Ngram search, "compassion fatigue" usage peaked in 2001, but the idea has been around for centuries. As the historian Samuel Moyn once put it, "Compassion fatigue is as old as compassion." In his essay "Empathy in History, Empathizing with Humanity," Moyn shows how philosophers and moralists in the eighteenth century who "rooted ethics in sentiment and sympathy" were troubled that "devoting oneself to an ethic of exposure and sensitivity to others' suffering (or of engagement and action to relieve it) might lead to a numbed ethical sense." It was this worry that emotional fatigue could undermine our morals that led Immanuel Kant to abandon sentimentalism for the categorical imperative—the unconditional obligation to do the right thing.

More recently, the journalist Dan Rather claimed that "empathy makes for wise foreign and domestic policy" and "our nation today suffers from a deficit of empathy." These are words he may have borrowed from Barack Obama, who once said that the empathy deficit was a more pressing problem than the U.S. federal deficit. Empathy, many believe, is vitally necessary not just for direct human interaction but also for global relations: We need it to solve the world's many pressing problems. But if that's true, what happens when the world wants more empathy than we can give? What happens when we run out?

The term "compassion fatigue" first appeared in print in a 1992 article by the writer and historian Carla Joinson.

While studying emergency room nurses, she noticed "a unique form of burnout that affects people in the care-giving profession." An RN named Jackie had recently lost her favorite patient, despite "desperate efforts" to save her. Ever since, Jackie had complained of "lingering feelings of helplessness and anger." Likewise, a surgical nurse named Marian reported going through a period of "despair and frustration" that almost drove her to leave the profession—until she started to practice a kind of strategic remove. Joinson credits the phrase "compassion fatigue" to a crisis counselor named Doris Chase, who told her that "some stress is unavoidable"—however, "overpowering, invasive stress can interfere with our ability to function."

Before it had an official name, something similar to compassion fatigue had been recognized in medical liter-ature. By 1980, the *Diagnostic and Statistical Manual of Mental Disorders* claimed that "knowing of others' trau-mas can be traumatizing." Though it was not yet well defined, there was a sense that proximity to trauma could itself be damaging, like secondhand smoke. This effect was sometimes referred to as chasmal trauma—"chasmal" as in chasm, the gap that trauma bridges across—sometimes as vicarious traumatization.

In the early 1990s, the psychologist Charles Figley took particular interest in the ripple effects of post-traumatic stress disorder, a nexus of psychological symptoms, in-cluding extreme anxiety and flashbacks, often seen in people who experience or witness a life-threatening event. Initially, Figley used the term "secondary traumatic stress" to refer to the PTSD-like syndrome that can result in health care workers such as nurses and therapists who are not victims themselves, but provide "empathic support" to the victims of trauma. (I can't help thinking of Scarlett O'Hara in *Gone with the Wind*, running out of the field hospital after watching a man beg a surgeon not to amputate without anesthesia: *I don't want any more men dying and screaming*, she cries, *I don't want any more*.) According to Figley, trauma more easily spreads to people like health care workers—not only because they're more likely to be exposed to the traumatized but also because caring is often inherent to their sense of self: empathy as a liability. Figley, who had served in Vietnam, went on to adopt and popularize Joinson's term and became a major advocate for compassion fatigue awareness.

If you've ever cared for a sick parent, or a sick child, you might recognize the symptoms of increased stress—the bad sleep, the bad moods, the bad stomach. I have experienced compassion fatigue as a caretaker myself. John has a chronic illness, and when he started getting sick, several years ago, we didn't know what was wrong. He'd be struck with sudden vertigo and trapped on the couch, panicked, for hours—during a vertigo episode, the whole room spins and you feel pinned down, as if by centrifugal force. On other days, he was too dizzy to drive, too unsteady to walk without a cane. Even more worrying, his hearing started fluctuating, the levels changing from day to day, sometimes better in one ear and worse in the other. This made his work particularly difficult; he was teaching college at the time. Throughout it all, he had roaring tinnitus, which he compared to hair dryers, vacuum cleaners, jet engines, sirens, and on one occasion a UFO landing. Some days he could barely hear anything, and it seemed that any day, he might wake up with no hearing at all, unable to work or even communicate, even with me. John was in his thirties.

Because he couldn't reliably drive or talk on the phone, I became John's assistant, ferrying him to class when he was well enough to teach, canceling his classes when he couldn't leave the house, calling doctors and insurance companies, driving to appointments. Of course, I still had a full-time job. More than I hated these new and sudden demands on my time and energy, I hated how easily frustrated I would get. When he asked for help when I was already busy, I'd snap at him, and then feel awful about it. Many nights we stayed up late, exhausted; we lay in the dark side by side, worrying and arguing. In the morning, I'd get up for work while he tried to get a few more hours of sleep; at my desk, I'd remember the tone of my voice, and the fear in his, and choke up with remorse. Over and over I'd vow to be more patient, but a few days later, I'd do it again. I did not want John to think he'd become a burden on me—but the circumstances were a shared burden. One rough morning, he said to me, "I'm the worst thing that ever happened to you." I started crying immediately. "*No*," I said, "you getting sick was the worst thing that ever happened to me; it's not the same." He looked skeptical.

"Stress" doesn't quite capture this era in our marriage; we felt terror and despair. I was afraid for John, yes, but I also felt alone, starved for compassion. I remember thinking (and maybe saying, shamefully), *I want someone to take care of* me. I was pouring all my emotional resources toward John, and it seemed he was hoarding his, spending all his feeling on himself. (And wasn't that natural? Aren't there times when we deserve to collect, rather than pay out, sympathy?) Stress, anxiety, and uncertainty can reduce our levels of empathy. But it felt more like my empathy was being used up faster, due to greater demand.

The effects of compassion fatigue on health care workers are real and documented. Left untreated, it leads to a reduction in quality of care, an increase in clinical errors, and high employee turnover. Caregivers take these symptoms home as well. They have difficulty connecting with friends and family, leading to divorce and social isolation. Accordingly, caretakers are instructed to monitor themselves for signs of compassion fatigue, using self-assessments to test their "ego resiliency," "self-compassion," "spiritual intelligence," and "post-traumatic growth"—or the "positive changes that some trauma survivors report as a result of the struggle to cope with traumatic events." In America, we seem to have a preference for these positive narratives; it's why, after a terrorist attack or other disaster, our leaders tend to claim it's made them "stronger than ever"—the Hollywood ending for real-world trauma.

To ward off compassion fatigue, or recover if it's already struck, caretakers are coached to follow established guidelines of self-care, which include physical, psychological, and social commitments such as maintaining healthy eating and sleeping habits, making time for relaxation and meditation, and building a social support network, including at least two people who can be counted on to be "highly supportive." (If trauma is communicable, one hopes those supporters have a support network of their own.)

"On any given workday, I'm interacting with many people who are literally having the worst days of their lives," says an acquaintance of mine who works as a hospice nurse. But she is conscious of the risk of giving any one patient or family too much of her attention and energy. "I don't try to put myself in my patients' shoes or try to feel what they're feeling (although this sometimes happens anyway)," she told me. "I need to maintain my emotional endurance by not using it all up now in my first years of being a nurse."

My day job is nowhere near that harrowing; I work in marketing. But when I try to keep up the work of an informed citizen, I, too, feel that my emotional endurance is being tested.

There's a sticky note on the wall by my desk that says BE AN ACTIVIST. It's been there so long I hardly see it anymore. I worry sometimes that I haven't paced my outrage.

Not long after compassion fatigue emerged as a concept in health care, a similar concept began to appear in media studies—the idea that overexposure to horrific images, from news reports in particular, could cause viewers to shut down emotionally, rejecting information instead of responding to it. It was the journalist and scholar Susan D. Moeller who co-opted the term "compassion fatigue" to describe this effect.

In her 1999 book, *Compassion Fatigue: How the Media Sell Disease, Famine, War and Death*, Moeller cites 1994 as an unusually apocalyptic year, one in which the news became a parade of disaster:

> "The Four Horsemen are up and away, with the press corps stumbling along behind," charged activist Germaine Greer, after a series of debacles in 1994, ranging from ethnic slaughter in Rwanda and Bosnia, famine in the Horn of Africa and an outbreak of flesh-eating bacteria in Britain . . . Sometimes, like in 1994 . . . it seems as if the media careen from one trauma to another, in a breathless tour of poverty, disease and death. The troubles blur. Crises become one crisis.

This much bad news drives the public to "collapse into a compassion fatigue stupor," writes Moeller.

Susan Sontag grappled with similar questions in her short book *Regarding the Pain of Others*, published in 2003. By "regarding," she meant both "with regard to" and "looking at": "Flooded with images of the sort that once used to shock and arouse indignation, we are losing our capacity to react. Compassion, stretched to its limits, is going numb. So runs the familiar diagnosis." She implies that the idea was already tired: Media overload dulls our sensitivity to suffering. Whose fault is that—ours or the media's? And what exactly are we supposed to do about it?

By Moeller's account, compassion fatigue is a vicious cycle. When war and famine are constant, they become boring—we've seen it all before. The only way to break through your audience's boredom is to make it feel real; each disaster must be worse than the last. And when it comes to world news, the events must be "more dramatic and violent" to compete with more local stories, as a 1995 study of international media coverage by the Pew Research Center for the People and the Press found. Natural disasters are media bait—the sudden danger, the biblical visuals of floods and flames, the human drama of heroes and first responders. Famines, on the other hand, especially in the early stages, don't make great TV.

Ad-supported media channels survive on attention, and this leads to sensationalism, images meant to shock: starving, bloated children; cities ravaged by war. But these images, by design, are upsetting, and eventually we turn away—a form of self-preservation. When a story's not hot anymore—in the 1990s, that often meant low magazine sales; now we'd gauge it by a lack of clicks—the media drops the story: "Even if the situation has not been resolved, the media marches on," Moeller writes. As Tom Kent, a former international editor with the Associated Press, tells Moeller, "We cover things until there's not much new to say." In other words, crises often get boring before they get better.

Speaking of another "bad year," 1991, Moeller reports

that the "short-term calamities," such as earthquakes in Central America and a cyclone in Bangladesh, "eclipsed the longer-term and ultimately more deadly disasters" of famine and civil war in Africa, in terms of both media attention and political and public support. These quieter, less spectacular disasters are an example of what Rob Nixon has called "slow violence": an insidious destruction that happens "gradually and out of sight." Harder to sensationalize, easier to ignore. Kent says to Moeller, "The question is: Do Americans care about Africans getting killed? And the answer is: Depends on how you write it." In this light, compassion is a matter of aesthetics. (As one CBS producer puts it, the audience is used to war movies, so "real explosions have to look almost as good.")

It's a problem that coverage of African famine is limited; it's a problem that the public isn't interested. But there may be a good reason for both, beyond moral decrepitude. In 1991, Moeller says, Americans focused more on cyclones and earthquakes than other, slower global crises because they saw the natural disasters as "one-shot problems with specific solutions." There were clear ways to help, finite amounts of aid that would make a substantial difference. Famine, on the other hand, had been going on for years, despite it being a cause célèbre in the 1980s, as evidenced by benefit concerts like Live Aid and charity records like "We Are the World"—which sold more than twenty million copies, raising $63 million for humanitarian aid in Africa. Had those efforts, one might reasonably wonder, not made a dent? And if not, how much good could more money and attention do? What if we're just more interested in problems we know we can solve, and solve in the near future?

Numbness or indifference to real atrocity must look, from the outside, like cruelty. But Figley's belief is that compassion fatigue, in the medical sense, stems from a desire to help. There's no compassion fatigue without compassion: The caretakers at risk see somebody suffering, and they want to reduce the suffering. But they can't always succeed. Compassion fatigue, then, is stymied compassion.

If caregivers are at risk because they give care to the traumatized, then empathetic news-consumers are at risk because they consume the news. Just opening Twitter on your phone or looking at the TV in a bar could be a form of secondary trauma: exposure to enormous problems you can't possibly solve. Perhaps you can help, but the difference that an individual contribution makes—placing a call, voting, going to a protest—often feels imperceptible.

In *The Science of Evil*, the psychologist Simon Baron-Cohen cites multiple studies that reveal an "empathy circuit" in the brain. These are the parts of the brain that are usually active when, for example, we see a needle piercing someone else's hand—the psych-study version of watching *Un Chien Andalou*, Luis Buñuel's surrealist film in which a man appears to slice through a woman's eyeball with a straight razor. (It's actually a sheep's eye.) I cringe and look away because on some automatic level I imagine it happening to me. In some sense, having empathy is a way of feeling compassion for myself.

Human propensity to empathy, Baron-Cohen claims, much like height and other traits, follows a normal distribution, the so-called bell curve. This means that a select few people have extraordinarily high levels of empathy— he offers the anti-apartheid activist Desmond Tutu as an example—while some at the other end of the curve have zero empathy—including psychopaths and people with narcissistic personality disorder. (My mother once told me she read that the two professions that test highest for psychopathy are surgeons and Buddhist monks—presumably because both require detachment. Empathy as a liability: a barrier to objectivity or enlightenment.) The fact that most people are in the middle of the curve, Baron-Cohen writes, suggests that "moderate empathy levels are most adaptive." He believes we can assume that evolution got it mostly right: It's better overall to have medium empathy than to be off the charts.

Average empathy will fail some of the time—we will fail to feel what others are feeling, as the hospice nurse put it, even if we try. And this may be a rational—or if not conscious, simply automatic—response. Empathy, like any bodily process, has a cost. Hunger would be meaningless if it didn't make you eat. What good is compassion if it doesn't translate into concrete, external action? It's rational to cut off the supply of emotion if it amounts to wasted energy.

Can compassion fatigue be avoided? Has it become more prevalent? I haven't found definitive answers. Searching

for solutions to apathy in the age of daily mass shootings, I found an article written by a family therapist in
November 2017:

> Can I be honest? When I read that half the victims of the
> mass shooting at a church in Sutherland Springs Texas
> were children, I paused, then turned the page, disgusted
> and angry. Not just at the shooter, but at the people who
> died as well. It's awful to admit this, but I can't shake the
> thought that people died because they refused to listen
> to social scientists who kept telling them that guns cause
> gun violence.

The therapist identifies his victim-blaming reaction as
a classic case of compassion fatigue, then outlines some
solutions to the syndrome. First, "Personalize the tragedy": "Read the stories of each of the dead and connect
with them as people, not nameless victims. This simple
act of reading their stories can maintain compassion and
protect us from apathy." (Can it, I wonder? This could be
effective for any given mass shooting, but if we read up on
the victims of every mass shooting, won't the hundreds of
details begin to blur together?) Second, "Be outraged . . .
Don't give into the desire to withdraw." (This one seems
like telling someone the solution to cancer is "Don't have
cancer.") Third, "If you are still feeling burnt out emotionally, look for a tragedy closer to home."

This last tip struck me as especially inane, as though
compassion were an end in itself. Shouldn't we fight com-

passion fatigue because we worry that paralysis and apathy will make the world worse? I don't hope to increase my empathy for its own sake, especially by way of nearby tragedies. In any case, the tragedies are there—John's condition has been diagnosed and, for now, is fairly stable, but that's what he would call a Pyrrhic victory; the condition is deteriorating and has no known cure. I have a friend whose wife is dying of cancer; they've had to pay for her treatment through crowdfunding campaigns. This isn't unusual. Everyone has their own local tragedy.

Moeller's book focuses mostly on international news, and why Americans find it hard to care about tragedies abroad. Foreign stories are underreported or packaged as clichés; the images are generic, and the analogies are stale ("Formulaic images 'label' a crisis so that it is identifiable"). All of this fatigues us. But now the apocalypse *is* close to home. In 2018, the White House does something appalling or embarrassing every day, and meanwhile it does nothing to halt the looming existential threat of global warming. We've utterly failed to address the emergency in Puerto Rico; seven months after it was devastated by Hurricane Maria, the entire territory once again lost power. It all feels local and immediate, but after a year of news addiction that left me with insomnia and heart palpitations, I'm starting to detach. I don't "desire to withdraw"—it happens of its own accord.

Moeller says compassion fatigue is not inevitable. I'm not so sure. I get 90 percent of my news from text, from written reports, not graphic, shocking images. The words alone are shocking, regardless of how impartially they're reported. But this state of being shocked feels *normal*; it's a fact I hold in my mind but don't feel in my body. I can't walk around with my mouth hanging open all the time. I'd like to follow the guidelines of self-care, to preserve my "emotional endurance," not as a professional caregiver, but as a regular person who cares about the world. So I take breaks and try to reduce my stress. I go out drinking with friends; I watch old poker tournaments on YouTube. But my breaks are getting longer. They feel dangerously close to avoidance.

That distance is better, I suppose, than feeling hopelessly enraged. But what is my responsibility? How much about global suffering am I supposed to know, and what can I really do with that knowledge? Social media, twenty-four-hour news, alerts on my iPhone—the demands on our compassion are much higher than a cave dweller or Kant had to contend with. It's overwhelming, even paralyzing, and very likely makes me less effectual in the local spaces where I might actually be able to do some good. Whether or not I personally keep up with everything happening everywhere all the time, I know it exists; that awareness alone is fatiguing. It's very easy to succumb to fatalism, perhaps the logical extension of compassion fatigue—believing we're "fucked" no matter what we do is mysteriously tempting.

Do we *need* to feel bad in order to do good? The psychologist Paul Bloom, who wrote a book called *Against Empathy*, argues, or perhaps hopes, that we can be moral without depending on empathy, which is biased and unreliable—we shouldn't dole out aid in accordance with the amount of sympathy we feel for people, he claims; we should help the people who need the most help. The answer, in Bloom's mind, is not to dial up our sympathy for everyone, to unsustainable levels, but to dial it down so that we can approach problems more logically. (He quotes Elaine Scarry: "Bring everyone to the same level by diminishing yourself. Put yourself, and those you love, on the level of strangers.") Even Baron-Cohen, who equates "empathy erosion" with evil itself, concedes that there are people with zero empathy (severe autistics) who are also rigidly moral; they manage this by systematizing right and wrong. This seems to indicate that good ethics don't depend on the feeling of empathy. However, most of us are not that systematic.

On New Year's Day of 2017, John and I invited an activist we know over for dinner, an older man who has much more experience in organizing than we do. While they talked and planned, I cooked and drank wine and grew maudlin. "Stop despairing!" our friend suddenly snapped at me. "That's not a *strategy*."

The next time I saw him, a couple of months later, he apologized for having raised his voice, and conceded that there are many forms of activism. "Maybe writing can be yours," he said. I had skipped several public protests in the interim, feeling I had too much other work to do. But I was heartened that people I knew attended. I liked the photos they posted on social media—I felt inspired by the size of the crowds, knowing others had the time and the strength to march in the streets for what we all believed. I remembered hearing that migrating birds fly together in a V because the shape is aerodynamic, saving them energy—the one in the front, at the point of the V, has to do more work, but when it gets tired, it falls to the back.

It's comforting to think that when we're too fatigued to fight, someone else will take the lead. It is, perhaps, too comforting.

2018

IN OUR MIDST

In 1954, the same year William Golding's novel *Lord of the Flies* was published, a group of psychologists at the University of Oklahoma performed a Golding-esque experiment. They selected eleven boys, between fifth and sixth grade, to live on a Boy Scout camp in Robbers Cave State Park during the summer. The boys were all eleven or twelve years old, of similar height and weight; they came from middle-class Protestant backgrounds and were seemingly well-adjusted, with above-average performance in school.

Over the course of the first week, the boys spontaneously self-organized, selecting a name for themselves ("the Eagles") and forming clear hierarchies. The researchers had expected as much. At this point, having bonded and tacitly agreed on their internal status, the Eagles became aware of an identical group of boys—eleven more, chosen for the same characteristics—who were camping in another part of the park. This other group had called themselves "the Rattlers."

The psychologists, led by Muzafer Sherif, had designed the experiment to test the hypothesis that "conditions of competition and group frustration" would lead to hostile relations. However, the Eagles and Rattlers instantly viewed each other as rivals—for no apparent reason. The tensions began before the researchers even created the conditions of competition. As one write-up of the study put it, simply overhearing the other group's voices or seeing their cups left behind on the grounds provoked "strong territorial reactions, such as 'they'd better not be in our swimming hole.'"

The boys, as though actively seeking conflict, started asking the camp supervisors (in reality, the researchers) to arrange competitions between them. Thus began Stage 2 of the experiment: a tournament between the camps. The winners were promised a trophy and other prizes. At their first face-to-face meeting, a baseball game, the teams shouted invective and finally burned each other's territorial flags. This led to an escalating series of strikes and counterstrikes. (*Lex talionis*: the law of retaliation.) The Rattlers raided the Eagles' cabin, tearing their mosquito nets and stealing comic books; the Eagles in turn raided the Rattlers' camp during dinner. The boys began stockpiling crude homemade weapons, like socks filled with stones.

The Robbers Cave experiment is a classic example used in realistic conflict theory, a social psychology approach that attempts to explain the behavior of groups competing over the same resources. But the Eagles and the Rattlers weren't battling over food or fuel or women, like tribes or nations in the real world might. And even before the competitive tournament began, each side saw their peers in the other camp—who might easily have been assigned to their own camp instead—as outsiders. It's not clear if this antagonism was inevitable. Is the distinction between "friend" and "enemy," as the German legal scholar Carl Schmitt believed, irreducible? Or did the psychologists somehow encourage the boys' warlike behavior?

In his foreword to a 2007 edition of Schmitt's *The Concept of the Political*, Tracy B. Strong notes that Schmitt "identifies as the 'high points of politics' those moments in which 'the enemy is, in concrete clarity, recognized as the enemy.'" The term "high points" recalls a frisson I associate with the morning of 9/11. John, whom I did not know at the time, was woken that morning by a phone call from his father, who said, "Turn on the news," and then, significantly: *"We're at war."* I, too, remember an agitated excitement around me, a sense of purpose gathering itself—an enemy taking shape. Perhaps the boys at Robbers Cave had a slight tendency toward conflict, the psychologists a slight tendency to foster it, and these tendencies compounded each other.

One year after the Robbers Cave experiment, in 1955, the anthropologist K. E. Read published a study in "comparative ethics" in the journal *Oceania*. It was about the Gahuku-Gama, a native people (or "congeries of tribes") in New Guinea. According to Read, the Gahuku-Gama do not subscribe, as Christians in the West do, to a form of deontological, duty-based ethics, where certain behaviors are considered inherently good or bad, and should therefore be pursued or avoided for their own sake. Their morality is more consequentialist, with retribution as deterrent: "Instead of saying it is 'good' or 'right' to help others, they state quite simply that 'if you don't help others, others won't help you' . . . disrespect for elders, lack of regard for age mates, failure to support fellow clansmen, incest or breaking the rules of clan exogamy all involve practical penalties."

However, the tribes do not apply this pragmatic, Golden Rule–like thinking to all people equally; the morals work only inside the group. "Gahuku-Gama assertions of what is right or wrong, good or bad, are not intended to apply to all men; they are stated from the position of a particular collectivity outside of which the moral norm ceases to have any meaning," Read writes. There is no universal moral law, then, no Kantian categorical imperative for the Gahuku-Gama: When it comes to people outside their tribe, "it is justifiable to kill them, to steal from them and to seduce their women." The value of a life, its worthiness of our moral regard, is determined by social relations. *The other* just doesn't count as much, or doesn't count at all.

What in the world are we supposed to care about, and how much? Do our loyalties belong with our friends first—be it our literal friends or, as Schmitt believed, our nation-state?

Or do we, as Emmanuel Levinas suggested, have "infinite responsibility" toward the other, any and every other?

On Twitter, I see arguments almost every day over the question of what deserves our compassion. Some outrages are seen as worthy, and others are deemed frivolous, a distraction from the more important problems. When you've been accused of focusing on the wrong issue, the simple shame-deflecting response is that we can care about more than one thing at a time. And we can. But I don't think the problem is entirely trivial—because we can't actually care about everything equally, especially not all at once. My responsibility may be infinite, but my empathy is not, and there is more evil in the world at any given moment than I feel physically capable of processing, much less addressing with due thought and care.

Many of my friends watched and live-tweeted Barack Obama's press conference on December 16, 2016. We had been wracked with fear since Election Day. We nursed secret, irrational hopes that he would denounce President-Elect Donald Trump, reveal something to prevent him from taking office, or otherwise somehow save us. Of course, he did not. It was a typical Obama performance, cool as can be—except for one emotional answer, where for a moment I thought he might cry. Mike Dorney of Bloomberg had asked, "Do you, as president of the United States, leader of the free world, feel any personal moral responsibility now at the end of your presidency for the carnage we're all watching in Aleppo, which I'm sure disturbs you?" Obama responded:

Mike, I always feel responsible. I felt responsible when kids were being shot by snipers. I felt responsible when millions of people had been displaced. I feel responsible for murder and slaughter that's taken place in South Sudan that's not being reported on, partly because there's not as much social media being generated from there. There are places around the world where horrible things are happening and because of my office, because I'm president of the United States, I feel responsible. I ask myself every single day, is there something I could do that would save lives and make a difference and spare some child who doesn't deserve to suffer. So that's a starting point. There's not a moment during the course of this presidency where I haven't felt some responsibility.

This answer has stuck with me, in part because the contrast to Trump was so stark. But I was struck, too, by the comment about South Sudan. My Twitter feed had been full of reactions to the news from Aleppo. Whether the horror was genuine or performative seems beside the point—like those studies showing that smiling makes you happier, fake horror probably encourages real horror, and drives real action. (I wouldn't have made a donation to the White Helmets, a volunteer organization based in Syria, if someone I follow hadn't tweeted a link, in the midst of the horror.) But as Obama said, hardly anyone I knew was talking about the civil war and famine in South Sudan.

Maybe we can care about nearby minor injustices, like a sexist commercial or racist casting in a Hollywood movie, and faraway great injustices like the bombings of civilians in Syria at the same time. But can we meaningfully, not just nominally, care about Sudan and Syria at the same time, or does this stretch the capacity of human understanding? We're not rational robots who always give our money and time to the best causes in order. Maybe Obama is capable of caring because he knows much more about both situations: comprehension as compassion. But how is the average, ignorant citizen supposed to conjure or ration this level of empathy, and do they have any moral responsibility to?

Social media, with its reach and immediacy, even intimacy, threatens the "us versus them" classifications we make so naturally. It exposes us to people who are suffering thousands of miles away. Moral people don't want other people to suffer—at least not visibly. But for most of human history, we were sheltered from knowing about suffering outside our immediate in-group. With a lower global population, there was less total suffering in the first place, but our ancestors also lacked the means of communication that now make it possible for us to *see* total strangers in excruciating pain, whether it's a video of a man being strangled by a cop in New York or journalistic footage of government-sanctioned murders in the Philippines. When that distance across time and space collapses, the concept of "the other" loses clarity, confusing our moral distinctions.

There's a richness of detail in the media of suffering that tests the limits of our empathy—if not asking too much, then asking too often. Empathy is a scarce resource; chronic stress has been shown to reduce empathy. Similar to "ego depletion," a phenomenon seen in psychology studies where overexerting one's willpower leads to a period of reduced will or control—like muscle fatigue for the self—we experience empathy depletion when exposed to excess suffering.

As the injustices pile up, and reserves run low, the question of where we should focus our moral attention becomes critical—when exposed to more evils than we can possibly attend to, most of us feel helpless. And what, more than helplessness, excuses apathy and inaction? Rather than confront global suffering, we may cull our feeds, or stop watching the news. Or, worse, we may make of the suffering other an enemy, turning apathy to antipathy. These unspoken algorithms by which we manage our empathy— they are almost innocent, almost "self-care." (We're not committing atrocities, just refusing to witness them.) But layered together, they have the shade of evil.

I am struggling to write about evil. I wrote and then deleted some seven hundred words—about the incoherence of ethics, the failure of ethics to scale from local to global, to work outside contrived philosophical thought experiments—because they sounded too certain. I am not an expert in international ethics, or ethics of any sort. But if ethical systems are incoherent, which I believe they are, wherefore my moral certainty? Perhaps I should write instead about my own participation in evil: my complicity and complacency as an American, and my entitlement. I ignore the evils that support my quality of life, to which I've become accustomed. We've arranged to make the evils that benefit us invisible.

I was in the midst of writing and rewriting this when I began to see reports of the missile strikes in Syria on April 6, 2017. This is the second time I've used the word "midst." I always think of a former colleague, who once mistakenly wrote "in the mist of our journey." The midst is the mist, the fog of war.

I wished John were home to discuss this new development with me, to help me decide how to feel. He was out teaching a class that night, using as course material Lucy Grealy's *Autobiography of a Face*, a devastating book by a woman whose disfigurement due to jaw cancer was the blight of her life. I felt her suffering no less keenly because it involved vanity. (Grealy died at thirty-nine of a heroin overdose.)

Once home, John sat on the couch with his laptop, getting caught up on what he'd missed during class. (A new feature of our lives: a genuine *fear* of missing out on some new piece of news, some life-altering change that's occurred while we're flying or while we're asleep.) I told him I was struggling with the essay on evil. He suggested I read *The Other* by Ryszard Kapuściński. When I googled Kapuściński, two of the first five results were about his questionable reputation. One headline, at *Slate*: "The lies of Ryszard Kapuściński—or, if you prefer, the 'magical realism.'" Another, in the *Guardian*: "Poland's ace reporter Ryszard Kapuściński accused of fiction-writing." Suddenly

I wondered if my essay about evil should cite only evil sources; Carl Schmitt was a Nazi sympathizer. How am I qualified to write about evil? Am I another evil source?

The author and filmmaker Laurens van der Post wrote a book about evil called *The Dark Eye in Africa*. The title is based on the Javanese term *mata kelap*, or "dark eye," equivalent to what the Malaysians call *amok*. In English, "running amok" suggests wild and disruptive but essentially harmless behavior; I picture toddlers at a birthday party. The original term is more specific, per van der Post:

> It is a phenomenon where a human being who has behaved respectably in the collective sense, obeying all the mores and the collective ethos of a particular culture and people, suddenly at the age of about 35 or 40 finds all this respectability too much—and takes a dagger and murders everyone around before being overpowered.

Van der Post uses this "darkening of the eye" as a metaphor for racial prejudice in South Africa and, by extension, for all the evils of war. The mistake we so often make, he contends, is self-exoneration: "One culture after another is still running amok and people are still murdering one another in the belief that it is not they but their neighbors who are evil." It's not that the other guy *isn't* evil, he implies, but that we are evil too: "Evil is a fact," he writes, basic and inescapable—"There is almost a sense in which evil is not evil!" Societal mores are in place not to maintain the natural order but to enforce unnatural order. The point is driven home by van der Post's own biography: After his death, a journalist, originally a fan of his work, exposed him as a statutory rapist and a fraud.

Again I remember the boys at Robbers Cave, who didn't need a reason to hate each other. Under the right conditions, animosity just emerges, like life from a muck of organic compounds. Schmitt believed that without the threat of being killed, life would be purposeless—that we define ourselves against an "adversary" who "intends to negate his opponent's way of life and therefore must be repulsed or fought in order to preserve one's own form of existence." He seems to suggest that meaning—in the form of engagement with evil—is a basic human need.

Sometimes I think evil is merely cumulative, an effect of scale, a swarm intelligence. If it was just two boys who found each other in the woods, wouldn't they band together, become friends? Or would they become a group in search of an enemy?

2017

EPILOGUE: THE UNREALITY OF TIME

I was listening to an episode of the BBC podcast *In Our Time*, on which a group of English scholars was discussing the French philosopher Henri Bergson, when one of them mentioned an essay called "The Unreality of Time," originally published in 1908, by a philosopher named John McTaggart. The phrase startled me—I was writing a book called *The Unreality of Memory*. It's possible I'd heard the title before and forgotten I knew it—as the scholars note, it is a famous essay. ("Is forgotten knowledge knowledge all the same?" is the kind of question we asked in my college philosophy classes.) In any case, I had never read it. I paused the podcast and found the essay online, curious what I'd been referencing.

McTaggart does not use "unreality" in the same way I do, to describe a quality of *seeming* unrealness in something I assume to be real. Instead, his paper sets out to prove that time literally does not exist. "I believe that time is unreal," he writes. The paper is interesting ("Time only belongs to the existent" . . . "The only way in which time can be real is by existing") but not convincing.

McTaggart's argument hinges in part on his claim that perception is "qualitatively different" from either memory or anticipation—this is the difference between past, present, and future, the way we apprehend events in time. Direct perceptions are those that fall within the "specious present," a term coined by E. R. Clay and further developed by William James (a fan of Bergson's). "Everything is observed in a specious present," McTaggart writes, "but nothing, not even the observations themselves, can ever be in a specious present." It's illusory—the events are fixed, and there is nothing magically different about "the present" as a point on a timeline. This leads to an irresolvable contradiction, to his mind.

Bergson, for his part, believed that memory and perception were the same, that they occur simultaneously: "The pure present is an ungraspable advance of the past devouring the future. In truth, all sensation is already memory." He thought this explained the phenomenon of déjà vu— when you feel something is happening that you've experienced before, it's because a glitch has allowed you to notice the memory forming in real time. The memory—*le souvenir du présent*—is attached not to a particular moment in the past but to the past in general. It has a past-like feeling; with that comes an impression one knows the future.

Bergson was hugely popular in the early twentieth century. He was friends with Marcel Proust—and married to Proust's cousin—and his ideas influenced many other modernist writers and artists. He is less well-known and celebrated now in part because of a years-long debate with Albert Einstein over the nature of time. Bergson believed that "clock-time" and what he called Time (with a capital T)—time as we experience it, a lived duration—were entirely different. It was this other kind of time, time in the mind, that interested Bergson. Einstein thought this was poppycock. "Il n'y a donc pas un temps des philosophes," he said on April 22, 1922, at an infamous lecture in Paris: There is no philosophers' time. Einstein felt his theory of relativity was the final word—time is what clocks measure, in their own frames of reference—and that Bergson did not understand the theory. Einstein thought the separation of time and space was dead as a concept, that he'd killed it. He was wrong—we still think of time and space as different, even if we grasp relativity. Nonetheless, many took his side, and it did lasting damage to Bergson's reputation.

Philosophers and physicists still speak of the specious present. "The true present is a dimensionless speck," Alan Burdick writes in his book *Why Time Flies*. "The specious present, in contrast, is 'the short duration of which we are immediately and incessantly sensible'"—he quotes James. The specious present, Burdick adds, "is a proxy measure of consciousness." It is what we think of as now. Not the general now, as in "the way we live now," but *right now*.

And how long is now? In an eight-minute YouTube video with over one million views, called "What exactly is the present?," the physicist Derek Muller attempts to explain. According to Muller, engineers working on the problem of syncing video and audio in preparation for the first live television broadcasts found that viewers didn't actually notice if they were a little out of sync, but there was "an asymmetry"—the sound can lag the video by up to 125 milliseconds before people notice something's wrong, but if the sound leads the video by more than 45 milliseconds, they know it's off. Of course, sound and "video" aren't synced in the real world either: When we watch someone walk down the street, away from us, dribbling a basketball, the sound takes longer and longer to reach us, but we still perceive the bouncing sounds and the bouncing visuals as simultaneous. That's because "now" is not a speck but a span, of about a tenth of a second. During that interval, Muller says, "your brain can perform manipulations that distort your perception of time and rearrange causality"— syncing up the audio and video, like a live broadcast on a slight delay. It's as though your brain takes in the information and processes it a little before *you* do. Researchers have exploited this discovery to fool people into thinking a computer program can read their minds, that it knows what they're going to do before they actually do it. We're capable of perceiving an effect before we realize we've caused it.

The neuroscientist David Eagleman has said, "You're always living in the past"—meaning not that the past haunts us, though it does, but that what we experience as the present is in fact the past, the very recent past, the just past. In a way, then, time is memory—not clock-time, perhaps. Not Einstein's time. But human time is human memory.

I started writing this book in 2016, in what seemed like a state of emergency. In the months leading up to the election, I was following reality like it was TV, as though every day ended in a cliffhanger. There was something addictive about Donald Trump's incredible rise—incredible in the original sense, unable to be believed.

This profound sense of unreality reached its culmination on the night of the election. Earlier that day, I'd felt light on my feet, optimistic—I risked jinxing it by purchasing proleptic champagne. I remember the moment, late into the night, when a win for Hillary Clinton had become vanishingly unlikely, though not technically impossible. John and I were watching the returns come in on his laptop, and stress-drinking, though not champagne—that stayed in the fridge. We watched a newscaster nervously talk through the maps showing Clinton's last outs. John turned and looked at me in horror and said, "He's going to win." A bottomless moment.

In the summer of 2017, I spoke on a panel called something like "Art in the Age of Trump." One writer on the panel insisted that the role of the artist is empathy; with an air of limitless patience, he suggested writing a story or a novel from the perspective of Donald Trump—to attempt to understand him. I felt a portion of the audience grow increasingly restless and frustrated. One man cried out, "There's no time!" I recognized the note in his voice, a note of urgency unto panic.

That panic, for me, has mostly passed. It has not passed for everyone—not for trans people I know, or for immigrants and the families of immigrants. But as scared as I am of the future, I must admit that for now I'm fairly safe, even comfortable. When news of another school shooting hits—the word "another" seems inadequate—or when I read calm, measured reporting of slowly progressing disasters like ice melt in Antarctica (or, or . . . I hate these placeholder lists of atrocities), I'm disturbed—logically I'm disturbed. I recognize the facts as disturbing, though what's no longer shocking or even surprising can verge quite horribly into boring. I still find Trump evil, but I no longer find him *interesting*. And I still have to work (how can it be so, that I have to waste my life this way, when the world is ending?), eat, sleep, and start over again. I move through the days in a flux of anxiety and denial. But that fear in the background changes things. It changes how I make decisions. I can't say how long this relative safety will last. It feels like a suspended emergency—like the specious present has been extended in both directions. *Now* feels longer.

Is the world ending? Which end is the end? For a while I told people, facetiously I suppose, that I was writing a book about the end of the world. Once at a family lunch, my aunt asked me what I was writing about, and I said I was writing about disasters. "What about disasters?" she asked, and I wasn't sure how to answer. My mother stepped in with a much better elevator pitch: "Isn't it more about how we think about disasters?" My own thinking, at least with regard to *the* disaster—*the* end—has shifted. To be clear, I do worry that civilization is doomed. (The word "worry" seems inadequate; I almost wrote "believe.") But I'm not sure the doom will occur like a moment, like an event, like a disaster. Like the impact of a bomb or an asteroid. I wonder if the way the world gets worse will barely outpace the rate at which we get used to it.

I don't have faith that my sense of history, from here inside history, is accurate, or that the view through the rickety apparatus of my body is clear. Eagleman notes that "most of what you see, your conscious perception, is computed on a need-to-know basis." We ignore what our brains—independently!—deem unnecessary. There is no other self, to tell your self what to do. The German biologist Jakob von Uexküll had a term for what animals pick up on in their surroundings: the *Umwelt*. The *Umwelt* is always limited by the organism's equipment, by its immediate needs. Eagleman, explaining Uexküll's ideas, writes: "In the blind and deaf world of the tick, the important signals are temperature and the odor of butyric acid. For the black ghost knifefish, it's electrical fields. For the echolocating bat, it's air-compression waves. The small subset of the world that an animal is able to detect is its *Umwelt*. The bigger reality, whatever that might mean, is called the *Umgebung*." The *Umgebung* is the unknown unknown, the unperceived unperceived.

There's the matter of perspective, and there's also the matter of scale. A young poet I know noticed that I often write about the self watching the self. He quoted an essay in which I wrote that I fantasize in the third person, connecting this to another piece, which mentions Robert Smithson's earthwork sculpture *Spiral Jetty*. "Do you think land artists moreso desired their work to be experienced within (standing on the rocks, beside the hole) or from above (via camera, airplane)?" he asked me in an email. My mind spiraled off. It's very hard for me, I told him, to be "present in the moment"—I'm always going meta, narrativizing, thinking about what I'm thinking about, imagining the future—and then in my specious present, I'm comparing what is happening to what I had imagined would happen, my *souvenir du présent* to my *memoire de l'avenir*. I didn't say that Smithson didn't mean for *Spiral Jetty* to be seen at all, or at least not for long—he built it when the water levels in Great Salt Lake were unusually low: a comment on ephemerality at epic scales. Finished in 1970, the jetty had disappeared by the time he died, in 1973, in a plane crash while surveying sites for a new piece. It stayed hidden for thirty years. Since 2002, drought has kept the water levels low, so it is now usually visible. The ephemerality doubles back: The design exposed, it's Smithson's intention, human intention, that's ephemeral.

I've grown tired of reading about disasters. Friends send me links, and I click them and skim halfheartedly. One article, published just after the Notre Dame cathedral in Paris was partially destroyed in a fire, references the sociologist Charles Perrow's 1984 book, *Normal Accidents*, which notes that safety systems increase the complexity of technology, inevitably leading to unforeseen errors, which can be catastrophic. The Chernobyl meltdown was triggered by a safety test. (In 2019, HBO made a series about Chernobyl, but I didn't watch it; I'm tired of disaster movies.) Another questions the slippery use of "we" in writing about climate change, as in "We are emitting more carbon dioxide than ever." "The *we* responsible for climate change is a fictional construct, one that's distorting and dangerous," writes Genevieve Guenther, a writer who founded a volunteer organization called EndClimateSilence.org. "By hiding who's really responsible for our current, terrifying predicament, *we* provides political cover for the people who are happy to let hundreds of millions of other people die for their own profit and pleasure." It provides cover, in other words, for the giant corporations, like ExxonMobil, Shell, and BP, that are responsible for most greenhouse gas emissions. In 2017, the Carbon Majors Report revealed that one hundred companies account for more than 70 percent of those emissions. "Always remember that there are millions, possibly billions, of people on this planet who would rather preserve civilization than destroy it with climate change," Guenther writes. "Most people are good."

That sentence gives me pause. "Most People Are Good" is also the name of a country song I hate: *I believe this world ain't half as bad as it looks*, the guy croons in the chorus. The more I think of it, the more I disagree. I don't think most people are good, or bad, for that matter. I think people are neutral. From a distance, they look almost interchangeable. It seems to me that "good people" can become "bad people" when provided the opportunity within an existing power structure—to claim and exert power at a deadly cost to others and get away with it. It is not an act of empathy for me to say that Trump is not inherently evil, but "we" have created opportunities for him to be evil. To say that most people are powerless—that evil is a role. In some novel I once read, one character reminded another that a "revolution" is simply a turn of the wheel; it doesn't break the power structure, it just changes who is on top. I think about that all the time. I think about these lines from an Ilya Kaminsky poem: "At the trial of God, we will ask: why did you allow all this? / And the answer will be an echo: why did you allow all this?" We, you and I, are not corporations, but we do give those corporations godlike power. "They" is a dangerous construct, too. There's no one to dismantle them but us.

I recently read my friend Chip Cheek's novel about a honeymoon gone wrong. It starts off feeling escapist—the publisher clearly marketed it as a beach read—but it turns into a kind of apocalypse novel. It's about what ruin really looks like; there are consequences for the couple's immoral (and stupid) behavior, but in the end we're denied the pleasure of an all-out catastrophe, the realization of what Sontag called our "fantasies of doom," our "taste for worst-case scenarios." The novel is set in the 1950s, but even period fiction written now is climate fiction, I realized; it's always on some level aware of what we've reaped. The storms have levels of foreboding.

My research into past disasters—the plagues and the almost nuclear wars—was often oddly comforting. We're still here, after all. But I can only take so much comfort in the past. This point in history does feel different, like we're nearing an event horizon. How many times can history repeat itself? It's generally accepted that our memories are fallible—that they're missing information, that they include new details we've simply made up—and that over time they are less and less reliable, as we keep rewriting the inaccuracies. We're more trusting, though, of what we take to be our direct experience, our experience of the present. I'm drawn to Uexküll's idea of the *Umwelt*; like a tick or a bat, we only know what we know. I'm drawn to Bergson's idea that perception and memory are coterminous. It suggests that we don't experience reality as it is, and then warp it in recall, but that even the first time we live through X, we are already experiencing our warped version of X.

2019

SELECTED BIBLIOGRAPHY

Adorno, Theodor W. *Negative Dialectics*. Translated by E. B. Ashton. New York: Continuum, 1973.

Alexievich, Svetlana. *Chernobyl Prayer: A Chronicle for the Future*. Translated by Anna Gunin and Arch Tait. London: Penguin Classics, 2016.

Anonymous. *The Incest Diary*. New York: Farrar, Straus and Giroux, 2017.

Bainbridge, Beryl. *Every Man for Himself*. New York: Carroll & Graf, 1996.

Baron-Cohen, Simon. *The Science of Evil: On Empathy and the Origins of Cruelty*. New York: Basic Books, 2011.

Barthes, Roland. *Camera Lucida*. Translated by Richard Howard. New York: Farrar, Straus and Giroux, 1981.

Bartholomew, Robert, and Bob Rickard. *Mass Hysteria in Schools: A Worldwide History Since 1566*. Jefferson: McFarland & Company, 2014.

Blanchot, Maurice. *The Writing of the Disaster*. Translated by Ann Smock. Lincoln: University of Nebraska Press, 1995.

Bloom, Paul. *Against Empathy: The Case for Rational Compassion*. New York: HarperCollins, 2016.

Boorstin, Daniel J. *The Image: A Guide to Pseudo-Events in America*. New York: Vintage Books, 1992.

Brooks, Michael. *13 Things That Don't Make Sense*. New York: Vintage Books, 2009.

Burdick, Alan. *Why Time Flies*. New York: Simon & Schuster, 2017.

Canales, Jimena. *The Physicist and the Philosopher: Einstein, Bergson, and the Debate That Changed Our Understanding of Time*. Princeton: Princeton University Press, 2015.

Canetti, Elias. *Crowds and Power*. Translated by Carol Stewart. New York: Farrar, Straus and Giroux, 1984.

Capote, Truman. *In Cold Blood*. New York: Vintage Books, 1965.

Cheek, Chip. *Cape May*. New York: Celadon Books, 2019.

Cohn, Norman. *The Pursuit of the Millennium*. Oxford: Oxford University Press, 1957.

Cole-Adams, Kate. *Anesthesia: The Gift of Oblivion and the Mystery of Consciousness*. Berkeley: Counterpoint, 2017.

Cusk, Rachel. *Outline*. New York: Farrar, Straus and Giroux, 2014.

Daudet, Alphonse. *In the Land of Pain*. Translated by Julian Barnes. New York: Vintage Books, 2016.

Dean, Carolyn Janice. *The Fragility of Empathy After the Holocaust*. Ithaca: Cornell University Press, 2004.

Dennett, Daniel C. *Consciousness Explained*. New York: Little, Brown and Company, 1991.

Diamond, Jared. *Guns, Germs, and Steel: The Fates of Human Societies*. New York: W. W. Norton & Company, 1999.

Dormandy, Thomas. *The Worst of Evils: The Fight Against Pain*. New Haven: Yale University Press, 2006.

Eagleton, Terry. *The Ideology of the Aesthetic*. Oxford: Blackwell Publishing, 1991.

Figley, Charles. *Compassion Fatigue: Coping with Secondary Traumatic Stress Disorder in Those Who Treat the Traumatized*. New York: Taylor & Francis Group, 1995.

Fromm, Erich. *The Anatomy of Human Destructiveness*. New York: Henry Holt and Company, 1973.

Fussell, Paul. *Thank God for the Atom Bomb and Other Essays*. New York: Ballantine Books, 1988.

———. *Wartime: Understanding and Behavior in the Second World War*. Oxford: Oxford University Press, 1989.

Garrett, Laurie. *The Coming Plague: Newly Emerging Diseases in a World Out of Balance*. New York: Farrar, Straus and Giroux, 1994.

Goldsmith, Connie. *Pandemic: How Climate, the Environment, and Superbugs Increase the Risk*. Minneapolis: Twenty-First Century Books, 2019.

Gooley, Dana. *The Virtuoso Liszt*. Cambridge: Cambridge University Press, 2004.

Grealy, Lucy. *Autobiography of a Face*. New York: Houghton Mifflin, 1994.

Harrison, Michelle. *A Woman in Residence*. New York: Random House, 1982.

Hecht, Jennifer Michael. *The Happiness Myth: Why What We Think Is Right Is Wrong*. New York: HarperCollins, 2007.

Hersey, John. *Hiroshima*. 1946; reprint, New York: Vintage Books, 1989.

Hill, Frances. *A Delusion of Satan: The Full Story of the Salem Witch Trials*. Cambridge: Da Capo Press, 1995.

Hull, John M. *Touching the Rock: An Experience of Blindness*. New York: Pantheon Books, 1990.

Ingram, W. Scott. *The Chernobyl Nuclear Disaster*. New York: Facts on File, 2005.

Irwin-Zarecka, Iwona. *Frames of Remembrance: The Dynamics of Collective Memory*. New York: Taylor & Francis Group, 1994.

Iskandrian, Kristen. *Motherest*. New York: Hachette Book Group, 2017.

Iversen, Kristen. *Full Body Burden: Growing Up in the Nuclear Shadow of Rocky Flats*. New York: Crown, 2012.

Kaku, Michio. *Hyperspace: A Scientific Odyssey Through Parallel Universes, Time Warps, and the 10th Dimension*. New York: Oxford University Press, 1994.

Kaminsky, Ilya. *Deaf Republic*. Minneapolis: Graywolf Press, 2019.

Keenan, Julian Paul. *The Face in the Mirror: How We Know Who We Are*. New York: HarperCollins, 2003.

Kohr, Leopold. *The Overdeveloped Nations: The Diseconomies of Scale*. New York: Schocken, 1978.

Kravetz, Lee Daniel. *Strange Contagion: Inside the Surprising Science of Infectious Behaviors and Viral Emotions and What They Tell Us About Ourselves*. New York: HarperCollins, 2017.

Kurzweil, Ray. *The Age of Spiritual Machines: When Computers Exceed Human Intelligence*. New York: Penguin Books, 1999.

Lappé, Marc. *Germs That Won't Die: Medical Consequences of the Misuse of Antibiotics*. New York: Anchor Books, 1982.

Levack, Brian P. *The Devil Within: Possession and Exorcism in the Christian West*. New Haven: Yale University Press, 2013.

Levine, Robert V. *Stranger in the Mirror: The Scientific Search for the Self*. Princeton: Princeton University Press, 2016.

Lindee, M. Susan. *Suffering Made Real: American Science and the Survivors at Hiroshima*. Chicago: University of Chicago Press, 1994.

MacAndrew, Craig, and Robert B. Edgerton. *Drunken Comportment: A Social Explanation*. Clinton Corners: Percheron Press, 2003.

Mackay, Charles. *Extraordinary Popular Delusions and the Madness of Crowds*. New York: The Noonday Press, 1974.

Malcolm, Janet. *The Journalist and the Murderer*. New York: Vintage Books, 1990.

———. *The Silent Woman: Sylvia Plath and Ted Hughes*. New York: Vintage Books, 1994.

Marías, Javier. *Between Eternities and Other Writings*. New York: Vintage Books, 2018.

Massimino, Mike. *Spaceman: An Astronaut's Unlikely Journey to Unlock the Secrets of the Universe*. New York: Crown Archetype, 2016.

McGuire, Bill. *Waking the Giant: How a Changing Climate Triggers Earthquakes, Tsunamis, and Volcanoes*. Oxford: Oxford University Press, 2012.

McNeill, William. *Plagues and Peoples*. New York: Anchor Books, 1976.

Metzinger, Thomas. *The Ego Tunnel: The Science of the Mind and the Myth of the Self*. New York: Basic Books, 2009.

Moeller, Susan. *Compassion Fatigue: How the Media Sell Disease, Famine, War and Death*. New York: Taylor & Francis Group, 1999.

Morris, Errol. *A Wilderness of Error: The Trials of Jeffrey MacDonald*. New York: Penguin, 2012.

Morrow, Lance. *Evil: An Investigation*. New York: Basic Books, 2003.

Morton, Timothy. *Hyperobjects: Philosophy and Ecology After the End of the World*. Minneapolis: University of Minnesota Press, 2013.

Nelson, Craig. *The Age of Radiance: The Epic Rise and Dramatic Fall of the Atomic Era*. New York: Scribner, 2014.

Nixon, Rob. *Slow Violence and the Environmentalism of the Poor*. Cambridge: Harvard University Press, 2011.

Osif, Bonnie A., Anthony J. Baratta, and Thomas W. Conkling. *TMI 25 Years Later: The Three Mile Island Nuclear Power Plant Accident and Its Impact*. University Park: Penn State University Press, 2004.

Parry, Richard Lloyd. *Ghosts of the Tsunami: Death and Life in Japan's Disaster Zone*. New York: Farrar, Straus and Giroux, 2017.

Perrow, Charles. *Normal Accidents: Living with High-Risk Technologies*. New York: Basic Books, 1984.

Przybylo, Henry Jay. *Counting Backwards: A Doctor's Notes on Anesthesia*. New York: W. W. Norton & Company, 2018.

Quammen, David. *Ebola: The Natural and Human History of a Deadly Virus*. New York: W. W. Norton & Company, 2014.

Rosenfield, Israel. *The Strange, Familiar, and Forgotten: The Anatomy of Consciousness*. New York: Knopf, 1992.

Rosner, Elizabeth. *Survivor Café: The Legacy of Trauma and the Labyrinth of Memory*. Berkeley: Counterpoint, 2017.

Sacks, Oliver. *A Leg to Stand On*. 1984; reprint, New York: Picador, 1991.

——. *Migraine*. New York: Vintage Books, 1999.

Savino, John M., and Marie D. Jones. *Supervolcano: The Catastrophic Event That Changed the Course of Human History*. Martinez: Paranoia Publishing, 2017.

Scaer, Robert C. *The Body Bears the Burden: Trauma, Dissociation, and Disease*. London: Routledge, 2014.

Scarry, Elaine. *The Body in Pain: The Making and Unmaking of the World*. New York: Oxford University Press, 1985.

Schmitt, Carl. *The Concept of the Political*. Translated by George Schwab. Chicago: University of Chicago Press, 1996.

Schweik, Susan M. *The Ugly Laws: Disability in Public*. New York: New York University Press, 2009.

Shorter, Edward. *From Paralysis to Fatigue: A History of Psychosomatic Illness in the Modern Era*. New York: The Free Press, 1992.

Showalter, Elaine. *Hystories: Hysterical Epidemics and Modern Media*. New York: Columbia University Press, 1997.

Sontag, Susan. *Essays of the 1960s & 70s*. New York: The Library of America, 2013.

——. *Later Essays*. New York: The Library of America, 2017.

Strawson, Galen. *Things That Bother Me: Death, Freedom, the Self, Etc*. New York: New York Review Books, 2018.

Trevor-Roper, H. R. *The European Witch-Craze of the 16th and 17th Centuries*. New York: Harper & Row, 1969.

Tuchman, Barbara. *A Distant Mirror: The Calamitous 14th Century*. London: The Folio Society, 1978.

——. *The March of Folly: From Troy to Vietnam*. London: The Folio Society, 1984.

van der Post, Laurens. *The Dark Eye in Africa*. London: Hogarth Press, 1961.

Wasik, Bill, and Monica Murphy. *Rabid: A Cultural History of the World's Most Diabolical Virus*. New York: Penguin Books, 2012.

Wright, Ronald. *A Short History of Progress*. Toronto: Anansi Press, 2004.

Young, Kevin. *Bunk: The Rise of Hoaxes, Humbug, Plagiarists, Phonies, Post-Facts, and Fake News*. Minneapolis: Graywolf Press, 2017.

Zinsser, Hans. *Rats, Lice and History*. Boston: The Atlantic Monthly Press, 1984.

ACKNOWLEDGMENTS

Some of these essays first appeared in other publications: "Magnificent Desolation," "Doomsday Pattern," "Big and Slow," "The Great Mortality," "Vanity Project," "True Crime," and "In Our Midst" in *Real Life*; "Threats" and "The Little Room (or, The Unreality of Memory)" in *Pacific Standard*; and "I'm So Tired" (as "Is compassion fatigue inevitable in an age of 24-hour news?") in *The Guardian*. Thank you to the editors who provided guidance and insights on earlier versions of these pieces: Nitsuh Abebe, Rob Horning, Nathan Jurgenson, Beejoli Shah, and David Wolf.

Thank you to the friends and friends of friends who offered me notes, advice, kindness, and other much-needed support as I worked on this book—I can't possibly name everyone in this category, but special thanks to Aaron Angello, Tyler Barton, Abby Beckel, Alice Bolin, Sommer Browning, Karl Chwe, Eileen Colwell, Erin Costello, Adam Jones, Adalena Kavanagh, Raymond McDaniel, Catherine Nichols, Jen Olsen, Kathleen Rooney, Martin Seay, Janaka Stucky, Laura Taylor, and Mike Walsh. Thank you to Matt Salesses for telling me he'd read a book of these.

Thank you, thank you, to my agent, Monika Woods, and to everyone at FSG, especially Jeremy M. Davies, Deborah Ghim, Devon Mazzone, and Claire Tobin.

Thank you to my extended family, including the Cotters, and especially my parents, Ann Gabbert and Michael Gabbert, for believing in me, challenging me, and being proud of what I do.

Thank you most of all to John Cotter, ever-present in my writing and in my life—as long as there are books and a couch to read them on, we'll be okay, we can be happy.

Illustration Credits

7   © AP Photo / Richard Drew.
24   "The patient's skin is burned in a pattern corresponding to the dark portions of a kimono worn at the time of the explosion. Japan, circa 1945." War Department. Office of the Chief of Engineers. Source: Wikimedia Commons.
71   "Trinity Fireball at 0.025 of a Second" © CORBIS / Corbis via Getty Images.
120 Courtesy of the author.
184 *The Ecstasy of Saint Teresa* by Gian Lorenzo Bernini, Church of Santa Maria della Vittoria, Rome. Photograph copyright © Joaquim Alves Gaspar. Source: Wikimedia Commons.